BUZZ, BUZZ!

BUZZ, BUZZ ! ESSAYS
OF THE THEATRE

CAPTAIN JAMES E. AGATE

Pol. The actors are come hither, my lord.
Ham. Buzz, Buzz !

BENJAMIN BLOM  New York/London

First Published 1918
Reissued 1969 by
Benjamin Blom, Inc., Bronx, New York 10452
and 56 Doughty Street, London, W.C. 1

Library of Congress Catalog Card Number 73-91309

Printed in the United States of America

THE criticisms of Sarah Bernhardt, Réjane, Vesta Tilley, Henry Austin, F. R. Benson, Weedon Grossmith, Laurence Irving, Pélissier, and the Irish Players appeared in slightly different form in the columns of *The Manchester Guardian*, and the Note on Stanley Houghton and the substance of the last three chapters of *Mr. Cleever goes to the Theatre* in *The Manchester Playgoer*.

I have to express my grateful thanks to the proprietors concerned for their courteous permission to republish.

Dedicatory Letter to
E. M. Baerlein, Esquire

DEAR EDGAR,

I take it to be fitting that this book should be dedicated to that one of my friends who, so far from being its only begetter, was the chief counsellor against publication. It was you who urged that the essential temper of newspaper criticism —its obligation to fire at sight—was antagonistic to reproduction. Little can you have guessed at the premeditation which runs before the critical impromptu ! Is it possible that you *never* had an inkling of the labour and travail which, with all good critics, should precede performance, that you took us at our written word and marvelled at the never-failing accuracy and appositeness of our instruction ? Whereas any honest critic will confess to the feverish turning up of *Little Arthur* which is to make him sound on the Henrys and the Edwards and so enable him to face the Histories without flinching, and to the furtive dive into the latest number of *The Lancet* which is to equip him for *Damaged Goods*.

But I also remember your criticism of such of these little essays as made their original appearance in a morning journal, to the effect that they would appear to have been written more with an eye to the approbation of posterity than to the enlightenment of a news-greedy public. In one breath you would have it that there is little to be advanced against the courage but everything against the stability of opinions primed and fired at two

Buzz, Buzz !

o'clock in the morning. In the next you are of the opinion that the finger was kept too long on the trigger. From which vanity might make flattering deductions as to certainty of aim, whereas you probably did not intend more pleasantly than that the work was laboured. Well, you cannot have it both ways, and I am emboldened to dedicate to you this little book in the hope that you will find the whole better than its parts.

One of the weaknesses of republication is the endowment of the original matter with a self-sufficingness and a self-sufficiency which, it may be hoped, was not its first wear. Nodules of criticism shy enough in their first inception now advertise a hectoring assurance and a lecturer's lucidity. Or say that they stand too obviously on their own bottoms, self-important and self-supporting as Mr. Crummles's tubs, too consciously aware of their obligation to arrest and convince the reader within the scope of a column, to expose their exact shade of meaning now or to be misunderstood for ever. Hence the arrogance and sententiousness which in the beginning were so much modest painstaking. The form, too, is become something of a bore with its wearying succession of beginnings, middles, and endings, the repeated driving of the nail home.

Well, better writers than I have taken these risks, and taken them cheerfully. Not one of the great critics from Sarcey upwards has thought fit to throw over the form in which his judgments first appeared. Mr. Arthur Symons is to be found writing : " I have frankly left all references to ' last week,' and the like, as I found them, because that

will help to show that I am speaking of a particular
thing immediately under my eyes." Mr. C. E.
Montague puts our case finely : " And yet for old
theatre notices there may be a kind of excuse. You
wrote them in a haste, it is true, with few books
about you, or moments to look a thing up ; hot air
and dust of the playhouse were still in your lungs ;
you were sure to say things that would seem sorry
gush or rant if you saw them again in the morning.
How bad it all was for measure, containment, or
balance ! But that heat of the playhouse is not
wholly harmful. Like sherris-sack in the system
of Falstaff, it hath a twofold operation ; ' it ascends
me into the brain . . . makes it apprehensive,
quick, forgetive, full of nimble, fiery, and delectable
shapes.' At least it sometimes gives you that
illusion ; below yourself in certain ways, you hope
you are above yourself in others." But the majority
of critics reprint boldly, without so much as with
your leave or by your leave.

I am therefore emboldened to present again
those actors of my time who have amazed or moved
or *tickled* me most. I beg leave to re-present them
as they showed themselves to me at the very instant
of amazement or emotion, that is to say, at the
highest pitch of our common excitement. For
readability's sake I have reclothed the criticisms
in a form in which they would appear to be the
considered and ratified opinion of to-day. Actually
they refer to particular occasion and are full of the
over-emphasis induced by the " heat of the playhouse." But as the over-emphasis is entirely one
of praise, it is, I hope, a pardonable fault. It is

Buzz, Buzz !

what the critic likes, and likes very greatly, that really matters. " Blame ! blame ! blame ! but praise, oh, dear no ! " said Dick Phenyl. I hold the contrary, I hold praise to be the first duty of the dramatic critic. I beg leave to re-present the actors in those parts which most urged the power of appreciation in me to jump to meet the power of portrayal in them. That is to say, that I have pre-ferred the quintessential to the encyclopædic, holding that an actor is better judged by his two or three great parts than by a multitude of moderate successes.

You used to say in the days of your champion-ships that you found the theatre an admirable relief. Hard thinking, you would say, is essential in the racquet and tennis courts, unnecessary, idle even, in the theatre. The ensuing pages will show to what extent I am in agreement with you. The point which will be elaborated and insisted upon throughout this little book is that theatrical criticism must not go bleating about the void, but must come down to the stern conditions of theatrical production as it actually is in this country at the present time. Under a system of government which neglects to clothe or nourish the bodies of young children but, as a great modern seer and prophet has re-marked, keeps them standing outside the doors of public-houses in the wet; under a tutelary system which registers our birth, half-educates us while we are young—I knew a stable-boy once who had a smattering of Euclid but had never heard of the Reformation—starves our old age, and huddles us at the end into a common grave, but never from first to last brings us into contact with Beauty, nor points a way which is not strictly material—under such governing as this there can be no hope for even so humble a finger-post as a State Theatre.

I may remark here that a theatre which should exist for the purpose of encouraging views on top-lighting or the use of stage-aprons would be a mere nuisance. A State Theatre exists for the performance of such plays as are by common consent or by picked judgment the best of our time and the theatre's history, but of which the production should be worse than unremunerative. We may think Ibsen's dramatic genius the greatest the world has produced for three hundred years, and Mr. Shaw's the most amusing but one. We are assured that the plays of Tchekhof are excellent on the stage, and we know Mr. Granville Barker's to be possessed of extraordinary interest. At the same time we are not surprised, in view of the mentality of the average theatre-goer, that the notice-boards with the magic words " House Full " are not always in evidence on these occasions. Surely a Government which is neither blind, deaf, nor asleep could afford to relax, at least momentarily, its pet hobby of baiting the brewer to run up a few State theatres, say one to every town of a hundred thousand inhabitants.

Were I the manager of such a theatre it would produce during its first three weeks Mr. Chesterton's *Magic*, Mr. D. H. Lawrence's *The Widowing of Mrs. Holroyd*, and Mr. Allan Monkhouse's *The Hayling Family*. And if, with adequate means provided by the Government, I produced these plays badly and with indifferent acting, I should

Buzz, Buzz !

deem it the critic's duty to pursue me with whips and with scorpions. But the actual conditions of play-producing in this country are quite otherwise. Put brutally, a manager who shall produce, not an honest tale of bawdry, but as much sly suggestiveness as he can get past the innocence of a Censor of Plays will make a fortune. The manager who shall produce *The Master-Builder* (Ibsen), *The Cherry Orchard* (Tchekhof), or *Fräulein Julie* (Strindberg) will lose one. And I hold the half-dozen plays I have mentioned to be among the finest of our time. I could mention another dozen, masterpieces all, which no theatrical manager without a taste for bankruptcy would ever dream of putting on his boards.

My first canon of criticism, then, is that it is not the business of the critic to take offence at harmless, or even harmful, drolleries. We are not the police. My second is that the critic shall deal gently with well-meaning effort, even though achievement be limited. There is never any harm in helping lame dogs over the right stiles. My third canon is that the critic shall not lose his temper because skulls are thick. The schoolmaster does not really get his proposition into his dunce's head by rapping on it with his knuckles. To sum up. The business of the critic is to praise the good wherever he finds it, in proper measure and degree, and not to find fault because it is not better. I hold a just appreciation of the *scope* of theatrical criticism to have so great a bearing on the general matter of my book that I propose to repeat what I have just said all over again in the very first chapter.

All this brings me, indirectly, to *Mr. Cleever*

Dedicatory Letter

goes to the Theatre. This little parable, fantasy, satire, or what you will, is to set forth the artist at his most inveterate, the critic at his most uncompromising—one who would certainly have denied any or all of my critical canons—and the *cabot* or *comédien* as he is understood in another country and as he exists in ours. I hope its extravagance may amuse you. It used to be the fashion in the days of our grandfathers to season tragedy with farce : " the whole to conclude, etc.," is to be seen at the foot of all old theatrical bills. Let me then kick up my heels at the end as though there were never a theatrical care in the earlier and more " serious " part of the book.

> Winnow, winnow, winnow all my folly and you'll find
> A grain or two of truth among the chaff.

But do not ask me whether the murder was " practicable " in the stage-carpenter's sense of the word, or what Cleever did with the body. You are to read the story as a parable of exorcism—of the spirit by the spirit. I would say this for Cleever, that he sees the theatre as it is, a box of tricks in which we may contain the whole world, and the actor as he is, a rogue (old style) with a halo.

A last word about the propriety of discussing in time of war matters lying outside the scope of war. The point I want to make is a delicate one, and I am anxious that you shall give it its exact value. It is that one may take the war too seriously. I do not mean that the soldier should be less than perfectly determined to give whatever may be asked of him, youth, health, happiness, life if need

Buzz, Buzz !

be. *But there was once an actor who took his Macbeth too seriously.* Life and death are not as portentous as this actor's shaking of the head and pawing of the air amounted to. In such a sense one may take the war too portentously. It is taking it too portentously—too brain-sickly if you will—to give up interest in all that makes peace itself worth fighting for. Don't misunderstand me. I hate your pacifist more than I do the devil. But to be perfectly absorbed in subduing the aggressor, to be entirely preoccupied with your mad dog even while you are preparing to destroy him, is to descend to Prussian levels of mentality. One has read of a brave soldier who a few seconds before he went cheerfully to meet death was deep in the *Maxims* of La Rochefoucauld ; of another who did not fall till, in the trenches, he had written poems that will live after him. If ever the day comes when war is to oust from our consciousness the things we knew life to be worth living for in the days of peace, then, on that day, we may as well sheathe the sword. The German will have won.

In remembrance of innumerable winter evenings spent with you and your lady round the fire in your old-world white and gold "parlour," the wind roaring in the chimney and the rain beating against the lattice ; in remembrance of your patient endurance of your old friend, of the slipping hours and our abundant talk, I dedicate to you this book.

J. E. A.

FRANCE, *July* 31, 1917.

Post Scriptum

I suppose it would have been possible to include the matter of this postscript in the general body of my dedication. But that would not have been quite it. My desire is to recognise certain indebtednesses in a place more likely to catch the reader's eye than among the fly-leaves, contents-bills, and other unreadable matter.

I desire to record a very considerable debt to Mr. Allan Monkhouse, Mr. C. E. Montague, and the shade of Charles Lamb. Whatever there may be of sanity or wisdom in this little book is due to the lofty temper of Mr. Monkhouse's published writings and unpublished unfriendly counsel. Whatever there may be of nattiness or felicity of expression I desire to recoil upon the brilliant genius of Mr. Montague, whom to admire is to imitate. These acknowledgments are in no way to be held to saddle these distinguished writers with whatever critical waywardness or folly the ensuing pages reveal. These qualities I contend to be entirely my own.

To Charles Lamb I owe my extravagant " idea of " the theatre, and it is by this magnificent reference that I would try to explain away a certain proneness to over-statement. To the majority of people the theatre is not an absorbing passion. So much the worse for the majority of people. I believe with Lamb—although for justification you must go to the spirit and not the letter of the essayist —that hobby-horses were made to be ridden—to

Buzz, Buzz !

death. You throw your leg over your business-animal soberly ; he is to outlast your time. But the pleasure-horse is to be ridden as hard as nag may endure and harder. One can always get down and walk. The theatrical hobby-horse is of all others to be ridden to a standstill. One can always come down to real life.

"I hate a lukewarm artist," says Lamb. I claim the merit of an equal hate.

Contents

Buzz, Buzz !

L'honnête artiste, cette infâme médiocrité, ce cœur d'or,
cette loyale vie, ce stupide dessinateur, ce brave garçon. . . .

BALZAC.

Buzz, Buzz !

ERRATA

Page xv, line 13, *or* " unfriendly " *read* " friendly."

"   27,   "   23, *for* " presentiment " *read* " presentment."

"   56,   "   12, *for* " Contras " *read* " Coutras."

"   94,   "   7, *for* " Brand " *read* " Branch."

"   109,   "   17, *for* " exquisitiveness " *read* " exquisiteness."

"   127,   "   26, *for* " heroes " *read* " hearers."

"   128,   "   8, *for* " Rabelaisain " *read* " Rabelaisian."

"   134,   "   8, *for* " *déclassé*" read " *déclassée*."

"   137,   "   26, *for* " all " *read* " ill."

"   167,   "   12, *for* " weds " *read* " loves."

"   187,   "   30, *for* " hock-bottled " *read* " hock-bottle."

I.
Little Lectures on the Art of Playgoing, with Some Considerations for Actors.

The Point of View

" CLEAR your mind of cant." The old tag may
well preface an enquiry into the whys and where-
fores of an art at once so direct and so elusive as
the Art of the Theatre. Perhaps the first piece of
cant from which we should free our minds is the
pretence that theatrical criticism is of any practical
use to either actor or public. Let me not be
misunderstood. I would not be supposed here to
be mounting the high horse of a plausible superciliousness, to be riding off on the æstheticism of
the 'eighties. " All art," said Wilde with his
regal scorn of the groundlings, " is perfectly useless." It is as well to note in passing that this
monarch of words was perfectly capable of bolstering
up his insecure and sophistical throne with the
most humbugging of pronunciamentos. All Art
is of course immediately useless just as Beauty is
immediately useless, and Wilde knew it. It was
his way of saying that no play or painting or piece
of music has yet succeeded in producing two pieces
of calico where one was woven before, and that if they
should succeed they are thereby disqualified from
æsthetical consideration. It is a barren case at best.

My contention that dramatic criticism is perfectly
useless is based on humbler and more literal grounds.
It is useless in the sense that it is no longer the
main instrument in making or marring the actor's
career. One of the evils of the spread of education
is the increasing confidence of the public in its own
judgment, even in matters for which a specialised

3

judgment is essential. I remember a plebiscite of the readers of the London halfpenny Press undertaken to determine the best piece of acting in London during a given year. The palm was awarded to a very competent actor, whom it is nearly always a pleasure to watch, but who on this occasion guyed and grotesqued his part out of all imitation of humanity. The critics had fallen upon the actor to a man, but not one line would he concede of a make-up as monstrous and as start-lingly unlike life as the simianesque attacks upon probability of M. Brasseur at his most farcical. The success of the actor in thus flying in the face of all criticism would seem to point to a new adage to the effect that whom the public are to like criticism must first destroy.

I cannot take entire objection to this. Part of my work in this book will be to show that the actor who pleases the crowd and who never fails to please the crowd *must be a fine actor*. The critic who should laugh himself sick and sorry with Little Tich or Mr. George Robey and then declare those exquisite buffoons to lack artistry is himself no artist.

Here let me tell a true story. I once had occasion to introduce to the theatre a North-Country farmer. The play was Sir A. Pinero's *His House in Order*. As my friend uttered no comment I was in some doubt as to the hold the play could be having over him. No word did he speak until we arrived at Sir Daniel Ridgeley's pompous " The

4

The Point of View

motor industry would seem to attract a good deal of the blackguardly element," whereupon my friend, who is a great horseman, whispered, " He's reet there, Mister ! " Silence again until we came to Nina's defiant " I go to no park to-morrow ! " Then did my rustic bang the rail in front of him with his fist and shout with the full force of his honest lungs, " And I wouldn't go to no b——y park, noather, Miss ! " Criticism can have little to say to an author exercising so strong and certain a hold.

Only once have I had evidence of the material influence of criticism on the actor. I had ventured to suggest that the accent on the word *despicable* might with advantage be placed on the first syllable. How great was my surprise to remark on a subsequent visit that the delinquent, a debonnair and knighted notability, had made so generous a concession as to thunder out, " Sir, your conduct is —dastardly ! " But this is the traditional exception. I have never heard of any other instance of criticism affecting so much as the lift of an actor's eyebrow.

And yet I must own that but for the spur and stimulation of the critical writing of the 'nineties the theatre had been for me an altogether commonplace affair. It is to the dramatic critics of that period that I owe the inestimable debt of theatrical wonder. Wonder at the peril and glamour of the theatre, wonder at its power to excite and purge— how often have I thanked thee, Mr. Walkley, for

Buzz, Buzz !

that Aristotelian word ! To criticism I owe it
that I still regard the theatre as a treasure-house,
a fairy realm, a world for belated children ; a world
in which voyages are still to be made as fabulous
as any undertaken by those romantical travellers
of my childhood, *Count Funnibos and Baron Stilkin.*
It is impossible for me even now to say more of a
great actress than that she can cloak herself with
the mystery of a Joanna Clack. I have managed
to preserve intact a *nursery* sense of the theatre.
So may it be when I grow old, as the poet said of
another wonder of childhood. There's a rainbow
sense about this early theatre of mine, if I could
only recapture it. On to this theatre time has superimposed a later one, a theatre for grown-ups, and
for the tired and nervous an inferno of paint and
terror. It is a theatre of Bobinot, *dit Bobinche,* in
which the bedraggled *Marthe* of Huysmans makes
her sentimental and tawdry début. It is the theatre
of sweating walls and leprous plaster, the inglorious
booth in which a Nana is a celebrity. It is the
ignoble theatre of the actress by courtesy. It is
the theatre of the single piece, " la pièce chaste,
un peu cochonne, avec une pointe de sentiment." [1]
Let us clear our minds of the cant that such theatres
as these are not " the theatre." They are ; and they
exist side by side with the childish one where
feathers are cocked, swords drawn, and flagons
drained in the true romantical, simple-minded,

[1] From Abel Hermant's devastating and ever-delightful *La Fameuse
Comédienne.*

6

The Point of View

and Chestertonian vein. And there's the glamour of it.

I have implied that part of my work in this book will be to discover the grain of beauty in the commonplace. But first I must be allowed to say a little more about myself, a liberty for which the author of *The Way of All Flesh* gives authority. " Every man's work," says Butler, " whether it be literature or music or pictures or architecture or anything else, is always a portrait of himself." For some account, therefore, *not* of myself, but of my first reading in a foreign tongue—a strange and foreign adventure consonant with setting foot in that other world of the theatre. My first adventure in French was the famous *L'Abbé Constantin*, an effort of the intelligence which was made to prevail throughout five and a half terms at school. My second experience—and I lump all these books together as one— was the three volumes of *Les Trois Mousquetaires*, the two of *Vingt Ans Après*, and the concluding six of *Le Viconte de Bragelonne*. The perusal of this epic may be said to have taken up my youth. I now come to the first book of discretionary years, the *À Rebours* of Joris-Karl Huysmans, famous or infamous according as one's appreciation of literary values is obscured by the prejudices of a temporary and topographical morality. If morality, as Butler averred, is made up of the custom of one's country and the current feeling of one's peers, if indeed cannibalism is moral in a cannibal country, then I see no reason to call *À Rebours* an immoral book.

7

Buzz, Buzz !

There may have been times and countries in which a Des Esseintes has passed for normal ; there certainly exist to-day hyper-sensitive and over-intellectualised beings with whom this strange hero will not pass for abnormal. I am inclined to agree with the dictum that " Art has no end in view save the emphasising and the recording in the most effective way some strongly felt interest or affection." Add dislike—which is as much a form of interest as affection—and this disgruntled romance must rank as a masterpiece. This book, then, I proceeded to take to my bosom, conceding with all the tolerance of eighteen years that it were better for ordinary mortals to stock their intellectual shelves with the naïveties of a " ventripotent mulatto " rather than with the misgivings of my over-subtle *détraqué*.

My first visit to the theatre was to a comedy by Tom Robertson, in which a milk-jug played an important part, and my second to a hole-and-corner performance of *Candida*. Again it occurred to my eighteen years that it were better for the world of one's elders that they should continue to sit under the milk-and-water predicator rather than expose themselves to the doctrines of a dangerous topsy-turvydom. My opinion was confirmed when, in response to a boyish demand for categorical elucidations as to the Rev. James Mavor Morell, his skittish creator replied that he was a respectable clergyman, but not thereby precluded from being a fool.

8

The Point of View

I cannot say that my later perfervid addiction to the theatre has greatly modified the views I first formed as to the relationship in which the average theatrical audience must always stand to plays of the order of Tom Robertson's and of the order of Mr. Shaw's. Since the average theatrical audience consists of a number of unremarkable people gathered together for a common performance, it necessarily follows that the theatre must make its appeal to those emotions which are common to every non-remarkable member of that non-remarkable assembly. Admitted that *Ghosts* is a finer play than *Charley's Aunt* and *Mrs. Warren's Profession* to be preferred to *Box and Cox*, but better and healthier for the general stomach I take it, the easier, simpler fare. By which I mean that poor fare which is assimilable is better than costlier provision which is not. Let me put it that if the theatres are not to be subsidised and are yet to keep open, the bulk of the fare must be of the simplest. From which it follows that your theatrical critic who would publish a *compte rendu* oftener than once in a theatrical blue moon, must in the very nature of things take his adventurous soul the round of the commonplace. The divination and discovery of the good in that commonplace, the making of distinctions on low levels is, in point of actual practice, ninety-nine hundredths of the critic's job on this matter-of-fact planet. And I hold such statement of the actual and practical scope of current criticism not to be a letting-down

9

of the art we hold dear, or a discouragement from a keen and brave appreciation of the subtle, the fantastic, the exquisite, and the rare. Whoso loseth his soul . . .

Lastly, let us clarify our minds on the score of art and morality. It is no æsthetic defect in the fine actor that he is not a fine fellow, just as it is no moral sin in the good man that he is an indifferent player. The old rhyme :

> As fiddlers they were bad, but then
> Consider what they were as men,

and Joe Gargery's

> Whatsume'er the failings on his part,
> Remember, reader, he were that good in his hart

put the contrary case fairly succinctly. The critic has to do with the artist who is an indifferent moralist. It is possible that there may be passages in this book from which a careless reader—and who would have the vanity to postulate a *careful* ?—might draw the conclusion that only bad men can become good artists or that art has such a contaminating influence that in her presence, as Shelley would say, good men are destined to become bad. Now it cannot be stated too clearly that Nature has not, so far as we can ascertain, laid down any such law or declared herself on the subject in any precise fashion at all. It is true that she has presented us with a certain number of isolated instances from which one may argue a certain tendency. Speculation on the subject would appear to be

10

fascinating since not only the moralist, but the
dramatist, novelist, essayist, and critic are never
happy unless they are having a go at what they
are all agreed is a very tough problem. We
may presume Shakespeare to have set the fashion
for our other moderns with his trick of gilding
only the weak and vicious with the glows of self-
conscious artistry. Dickens—to take a biggish leap
—had no doubt as to the typicalness of his Harold
Skimpole. Hugh Voysey (Mr. Granville Barker)
complains that his gift of vision is barred by the
respectability of his family. D'Annunzio's most
beautiful play is written round the disabilities
attaching to the drawing of inspiration from a
mistress rather than a wife. In Ibsen the characters who bother themselves about the arts are
invariably humbugs or hypocrites or *noceurs*, and it
would not surprise us to hear that Alving *père* had
a nice taste in engravings. Mr. Shaw would have
us choose between a world of good men and bad
pictures and a world of good pictures and bad men.
The cardinal fault of these romancers is their
passion for moral book-keeping. They will insist
upon taking our virtues and our vices to account.
Whereas I venture to declare myself against the
ineffectual striking of moral balances or the practi-
cability of keeping any such inquisitorial books
at all. You cannot measure triangles against
blueness, a piece of critical perception which I
have quoted elsewhere and shall probably go on
quoting whenever these questions arise. Even

Buzz, Buzz !

though the measures, scales, or other fourth-dimensional apparatus were to hand, there are still some very nice considerations involved. What is to be done with the young genius who sows his wild oats in a thoroughly practicable way, but never balances the account by reducing his undoubted genius to canvas, manuscript, or score ? It is to be noted that your moralist will always fight shy of the admittedly great artist who is also a back-slider. In these cases he will burke the issue, talk of Jekyll and Hyde, or declare that if the great man had been less wicked his most perfect work would have been more perfect, which is, of course, nonsense. Confronted with Baudelaire, Verlaine, Huysmans, Poe, or Wilde, and challenged to deny that the sole source of inspiration of these sick men is their very sickness, and that a return to health would have restored them out of existence altogether, he will reply that he does not read Baudelaire, Huysmans, Poe, and Wilde, and that of Verlaine his knowledge is confined to the so-called Poems of Wisdom only.

Looking at the question straight in the face—unlike the moralist who views all questions from an angle of prejudice—there would seem to be no very compelling reason why we should expect good men—" good " in the technical sense of non-dissolute—to provide us with good pictures. We rely upon them to do almost everything else ; to be faithful to their wives, to go home betimes, to be honourable in business, to " earn a little money and spend a little less," as Stevenson cannily put it in his morning petition—but there is no obligation on them to meddle with matters beyond their scope.

Be good, sweet maid, and let who will be clever

is a stupidity. Let who *can* be clever would at least have had the virtue of a platitude. But there is every reason why the world's bad men—bad in the technical sense of licentious—should be able to supply the world with good artists. You cannot pay Sobriety and Self-Control all the chaste and chilly compliments and then look to them for the phenomena proper to the temperamental volcano. All works of art are in the nature of volcanic eruptions. This is one of the things which no moralist ever understands and which no artist ever questions. To discuss it at all is really rather tedious.

But my whole point is that even the observed tendency of art to run in temperamental grooves must not be exalted into anything so definite as a Law. We cannot get over the fact that there *are* inexplicable things in this world. Three will not go into ten with anything like sufficient exactness to satisfy your moral stickler ; leave is given by the strictest to suppose so manifest an absurdity as a line so long that it can never have begun and so long that it can never end. Strange bodies have been seen hurtling through the air along a path which can never bring them back into our ken, and which can hardly, according to the laws of human reckoning, have brought them within the

13

Buzz, Buzz !

scope of our System at all. Nature has still her secrets. Why, then, should not this little perplexity of ours remain a decent mystery ?

> Cherchez les effets et les causes,
> Nous disent les rêveurs moroses.
> Des mots ! des mots ! cueillons les roses,

sings De Banville.

> Take the goods the gods provide thee,
> Lovely Jerry, sit beside me,

is our English version. We do not ask of the good man non-pertinent questions as to his power to paint the sunset. Neither should we ask of the good artist non-pertinent questions as to his moral conformity. Let us be grateful for good pictures whatever the faults of their fashioners. This will at least be a set-off against the consideration extorted from the world by dullards who have done nothing to amuse it.

The Actor as Visionary

A STATE of ecstasy is to be reckoned among the more generous lapses, an error on the magnificent side.   Writes the great French poet of his brother-visionaries :

Tous nos palais sous eux s'éteignent et s'affaissent ;
Leur âme à la coupole où leur œuvre reluit
Revole, et ce ne sont que leurs corps qu'ils nous laissent.

Notre jour leur paraît plus sombre que la nuit ;
Leur œil cherche toujours le ciel bleu de la fresque,
Et le tableau quitté les tourmente et les suit.

Comme Buonarotti, le peintre gigantesque,
Ils ne peuvent plus voir que les choses d'en haut,
Et que le ciel de marbre où leur front touche presque.

Sublime aveuglement ! magnifique défaut ![1]

A pardonable blindness, a magnificent fault, you may say, when levelled against a Michael Angelo ; less easily pardonable when charged to the account of the mountebank and vagabond.   Which of these notoriety-mongers, you will ask, was ever blind

---

[1] Our palaces founder beneath their feet ;
Their soul clings to the dome of their immortal work,
To us on earth they bequeath their material bodies.

Our day is darker than their night ;
Continually they turn their eyes to the frescoed blue,
The picture's torment pursues them.

Like Buonarotti, giant among painters,
Their eyes behold only the heavens
And the marble sky to which their foreheads lean.

Magnificent blindness ! fault ineffable !

The lines are taken, of course, from Théophile Gautier's famous *Terza rima*, in which the poet describes how Michael Angelo, when he had finished painting the Sistine Chapel, was unable to lower his arms.   The verse in the original, like all of Gautier's, has the purity of white marble, and I submit this crude version with the gravest misgiving.

except to his own artistic deficiencies, or less than supremely awake to the crowd yoked to his triumphal car ?

In the arts it is not always easy to give plain answers to plain questions. Criticism of the actor would be simpler were it not for the rehearsed quality of his emotion. At the moment of delivery the actor is essentially less interested than the spectator. It is not to be thought that the pre-occupation of Buonarotti when he descended the scaffolding of the Sistine Chapel was less than the wonder of the first beholder ; it is unthinkable that the great Dumas, rushing in tears out of his study with the exclamation, " J'ai tué Porthos ! " was less moved than his reader. But the Othello whose demand to be roasted in sulphur and washed in liquid fire should be heart-felt would not be able to sustain his rôle for a week. We may have to refer again to this old paradox of the insincerity of acting. As for its vulgarity, look around. Look around not, for politeness' sake, at the living but at the illustrious dead. Consider the departed glory of renowned actresses little other than courte-sanes, some indeed not so warm-hearted ; consider the luxury and insolence, the selfishness and feather-headedness—*étourderie* is the word—let the poet soften these vices as he may.

> Cœur d'ange et de lion, libre oiseau de passage,
> Espiègle enfant ce soir, sainte artiste demain.

Consider whether, on hearing of an actor that he

was a shy and modest gentleman, courteous towards others and a stranger to show and vanity, we should not on this report decide against him as a world-shaking virtuoso. And whether, on hearing of another that he was ill-mannered, vicious, moody, raffish, impulsive, ostentatious, egotistical, vain, we should be astonished to learn that he was, in the old phrase, an ornament to the stage. The French accept this contradiction readily. Let but a man prove wanting in honour, faith, friendship, and common honesty, and they cheerfully proclaim him *un comédien*. And the proclamation is held to be dispensatory of all necessity for further judgment. The category suffices. We English are convinced something against our will of this divorce of genius from character. " The most tragic thing in the world," says. Mr. Shaw's bedside *raisonneur*, " is a man of genius who is not also a man of honour." And yet when we read of Fanny Kemble and Rachel, we claim for the Victorian lady that she was a charming and gentle actress, and grudgingly admit for the Frenchwoman that she could undoubtedly play *Phèdre*. With all this, the French reverence for the actor's art is undoubtedly greater than our own, though they make short work of any pretensions of the actor in his private capacity. We knight our rogues and vagabonds ; the French dub them *cabotins*, with all that word expresses of tawdry finery and fifth-rate plumage.

" What reasons, then, can you give for claiming

Buzz, Buzz !

a state of spiritual ecstasy for your mountebank ? "
is a question one must be prepared to answer. I
am inclined to say of this suspect and theatrical
ecstasy what I would say of all the other artistic
elations—that it is the original ecstasy of creation,
all great acting being creative in the sense that if
there is one glory of Dickens' *Micawber* and another
decided and distinct glory of the same gentleman
according to Phiz, so also is there one glory of
Molière's *Bourgeois Gentilhomme* and another of
Coquelin's *M. Jourdain*. By ecstasy I mean the
original creative energy, imaginative fire, and
thought of a first fashioning, the laying-up in the
actor's brain of a first store of imaginative effort
from which to supply the minute doles required
of mechanical performance. This quantity of
imagination is constant, since the amount of renewed
feeling which the actor necessarily brings even to
rehearsed delivery can be relied upon to make
good the wastage of original treasure.

And how, it may be asked, is this creation of
original ecstasy so determined that we may be sure
as to its being a matter of imaginative fire and
quickening thought and not merely of careful
diligence and assiduity ? It will save a good deal
of trouble if we lay it down once and for all that
hard work by itself will no more kindle imaginative
fire than the taking of pains, however infinite, will
add up in the end to a score of genius. Whatever
the rude sage may have said, genius was never the
affair of accountancy. On the other hand, imagina-

tion is powerless without technical training. I do not know which is the more deplorable spectacle, the London leading-lady who has learnt to fold up a parasol, sink into a chair, and preside over the tea-cups with a distinction of manner concealing an intelligence less than a *midinette's*, or the actress so taken up with her spirituality that she has scorned to learn the mechanical business of walking across the stage. The old tag that Garrick "stepped upon the stage a master of his art" is responsible for an enormous amount of mischief in its encouragement to the actor to believe that he may rival Garrick by sheer virtuosity of the intelligence. Whereas the plain truth is that with the business of acting, the sheer power of pretending to be somebody else, brains never have had and never will have anything to do. Wherever the theorist writes "intellect" it is safe to read "temperament." There is a little verse by Théodore de Banville which exemplifies this need for technical preparation :

Sculpteur, cherche avec soin, en attendant l'extase,
Un marbre sans défaut pour en faire un beau vase . . .

In other words, the actor must busy himself with furbishing up his technical armoury *en attendant l'extase*, awaiting such time as it shall please the divine fire to descend upon him.

To define the flame of ecstasy is to go back to the first principles of all art. Shortly we may allege the passionate quest for beauty ; the search for light that never was on sea or land ; the expression

Buzz, Buzz !

of all that some mysterious madness has taught the artist to be supremely worth while setting down in word or paint or sound ; the effort to perpetuate beyond the grave and in terms of his art that consciousness of the world about him which has been said to be civilised man's " marvel and treasure." It is the love of work brought to perfection in a garret and on a crust. It is persistence in the face of neglect. Fame and applause are fuel to the vanity of the artist ; the flame of ecstasy burns a spiritual oil. There is no tragedian of the Shakespearean stage, no comedien ripe with Molière and charged with character like a bursting grape, no maker of faces at the Palais-Royal who has not lighted his lamp at this serene and steady light.

And yet there is something of the Will o' the Wisp about this ecstatic candle of ours. We must be careful not to allow the actor who has failed to master the elementary tricks of his profession to humbug us by hiding his incompetence under a bushel of pretended ecstasy. The audience has nothing to do with the communings between the actor and his familiar ; they are purely the actor's affair. It may even be that where the actor is most consciously ecstatic he is least successful. There was a distinguished player once who professed inability to deliver Vincentio's

> Look, the unfolding star calls up the shepherd,

unless he first visualised Watts' picture of Hope. To which a critic replied that the spur and inspira-

The Actor as Visionary

tion of the actor are irrelevant, and that the business
of acting, like the plumber's, is satisfactory only
in so far as it is practical. "What the plumber
thinks about is no concern of ours, until he trans-
lates it into terms of pipes." Between these two
extremes ecstasy must find a mean.

Perhaps it will help to an understanding if we
consider ecstasy on a humbler level. Once in a
sporting paper I happened on a definition which all
the thinking I have done since has not been able to
better. The writer was describing a Welsh pony:

A veritable Ganymede in form, this Shooting Star has
action which, when seen, makes life easier for the man who
loves fine horses and fine action.

This is badly phrased; the words "when seen"
are unnecessary, but "makes life easier" is a gem.
Makes life easier, there's the whole secret! The
action of one little pony made life easier for this
penny-a-liner, made him for the rapturous moment
indifferent to ill-health, bankruptcy, the world's
peace even. It is the business of great actors to
make life easier. There is an old saying which
describes people as being above themselves, and
Mr. Galsworthy has given his charwoman a phrase
for her drunken husband—"He isn't himself." The
business of great acting is to raise the spectator above
himself, to intoxicate him, so that he is no longer
himself but is raised to a power of appreciation un-
dreamed of in his sober senses. In this way the ecstasy
in the artist speaks to the ecstasy which is in all of us.

Buzz, Buzz !

It does not do to lay down too hard and fast a rule as to what shall or shall not elate a man above his normal self. The old Yorkshire proverb that there are trimmings for all sorts of cloth and buttons for fustian is true of the things of the spirit also. You cannot predict what will make life easier for the individual. I have been present at camp concerts where soldier-sentiment has stirred one's *heart* more than the masterpieces. I have seen an arch and fleshy singer—oh, the archness of forty ! —hold in cathedral silence a crowded music-hall notoriously profane. I have seen two plump females and a dress-coated counter-jumper, halo'd with blue, amber, and pink lights, draw with trombone, flute, and violin more tears from Godard's " Berceuse " than ever that sentimental gentleman dreamed of putting into it. All these trumpery ballads made life easier for many simple souls. They have as good a right to be considered challenges to ecstasy as, in different degree, the clown twisting his apron as the curtain falls on *Sumurûn*, the negro page in *Rosenkavalier* prolonging the melody by a strain that he may pick up the dropped handkerchief, Samuel Butler's likening of Handel's " And the government shall be upon his shoulder " to the shoulder of the Wetterhorn, the *Holà ! holà ! que fais-tu là à la fenêtre ?* of Sarah Bernhardt in *Pelléas et Mélisande*. It is the business of criticism to discriminate between these ecstasies, without superciliousness and without losing its head.

The Actor as Charlatan

IF, then, the attitude of the actor towards his creation is properly one of reverence, it is fitting that in his turn the spectator should abase himself before the glorious conception. But it is in no way desirable that the spectator should prostrate himself before the actor in the flesh. In the immensely amusing *Les Grotesques de la Musique* of Hector Berlioz—a sane and witty corrective which should be at the elbow of every critic—there is a long description of the attitude towards its favourites assumed by the public of that day. Berlioz postulates an admirer of Jenny Lind who, with some notion of preserving at least an appearance of mental balance, should indulge in no more extravagant a pæan than " Goddess, I am to implore your pardon on behalf of a stunted humanity for its inability to find words adequate to its emotions. Your voice has the sublimity of the Heavenly Choir ; your beauty is beyond compare, your genius boundless, your trill more amazing than the sun. Saturn's ring is unworthy to crown your head. Before you humanity can but prostrate itself ; deign at least that it embrace your feet." In reply to which poverty-stricken meed of praise the incensed *diva*, with a shrug of her beautiful shoulders, demands, " What noodle have we here ? "

The diarist, claiming for the great Kean's *Sir Giles Overreach* that it caused maidens to swoon and matrons to be untimely delivered in the pit did no more than faintly adumbrate the belief of

Buzz, Buzz!

world-shaking actors in their power actually to shake the world. We may, if we like, attribute this megalomania to the fleeting nature of the actor's triumph and his desire to seize the palm while yet it may be worn. Far from playing for posterity, far even from envisaging the considered verdict of the morrow, the actor demands the instantaneous applause of the moment. He who is to shake worlds must scatter his thunder-bolts within three feet of his judges, shut up with them in the stuffy box of false sentiment and vitiated atmosphere which is the theatre.

We might take a more charitable view of the actor were his art other than a calculated simulation, a rigorous abstention from the stimulant which it is his business to administer critically, in rehearsed doses, maintaining behind that false face of his an air of eager participation. The actor is a giver of banquets of which it is the prime condition that the host shall starve. Needs must, to borrow a phrase from Lamb, that he " sit esurient at his own table." " We're doing the trick, Charles, we're doing the trick ! " whispered towards the close of his career by the elder Kean to the younger in I know not what pathetic play of stage-father kneeling to stage-son, is good enough to be the classic instance of ecstasy laughing up its sleeve— charlatanism, in a word. To be reckoned amongst the most poignant demonstrations of the pathos of human intercourse, and amongst the most intolerable exhibitions measured in any scale of

The Actor as Charlatan

æsthetic propriety, was the last public appearance
of that always capable and occasionally exquisite
actor, Frank Rodney, stricken with a mortal complaint. The impropriety, the " charlatanism," consisted in the dying man's choice for his farewell
of the rôle of Buckingham in *Henry VIII.* :

> You few that loved me,
> And dare be bold to weep for Buckingham,
> His noble friends and fellows, whom to leave
> Is only bitter to him, only dying,
> Go with me, like good angels, to my end,

drew forth no tears for Buckingham, although
every eye in the house was wet for Rodney. At
the last words :

> All good people,
> Pray for me ! I must now forsake ye : the last hour
> Of my long weary life is come upon me.
> Farewell :
> And when you would say something that is sad,
> Speak how I fell. I have done ; and God forgive me !

men and women cried openly and the house was
choked with heartfelt and unlawful sobs. . . .

Actors themselves are the first to recognise that
the doubling of substance and shadow is not closer
than that of tragedian and buffoon. A great French
actress, wearied by a young gentleman's com-
mendations of l'Aiglon's dying cry of " Maman ! "
exclaimed with just impatience :

" Mais, mon petit, vous avez bien remarqué qu'à ce
moment-là tout le monde pleure, tousse, crache, se mouche
et cetera, et cetera. Eh bien ! je le fais exprès pour avoir
un instant de repos ! "

Buzz, Buzz !

A charming actress, whose art is as English as the heroines of Shakespeare, condemned on occasion to some crude drama of the Terror, is ushered into a room overlooking the place of execution. In luxurious abandonment to the most trying emotions —a scene of poignant dissembling—she awaits in agony the advent in the tumbrils of the greater part of her family. To her enters an attendant saying, " This, Madam, is your apartment." Through tears, and in a voice which has melted continents, came on one light-hearted occasion the *sotto voce* reply, " I trust there are the usual conveniences ! " Is it to be supposed that by such levity and " insincerity " the actress is to forfeit one-millionth shade of a degree of our reverence ?

One of our prettiest boy-actors, called upon to play the most talkative death-scene of the modern stage, is confronted towards the end of the sentimental agony with a veritable mouthful of a word. Young genius has no doubt about its proper course and takes the word in its stride. A bespectacled critic, peering into the boy's handsome face, enquires whether he would be correct in attributing this calculated gabble to a dying man's impatience with the slow machinery of speech. To whom the young artist says genially :

" Rot, my dear fellow, rot ! It's a beastly word anyhow and "—in response to a bewildered and sceptical shake of the head—" *I had no idea that I rushed it !* A trick of the trade, I suppose ! "

The Actor as Charlatan

It was the same young gentleman who invited a friend to the play, overcoming his friend's objection that he was engaged to dinner by saying simply, " My dear boy, I'm not on till 9.25. Nothing doin', first act ! "

And yet this lively fellow who would time himself like a performing fowl could do as beautifully and pathetically as any actor of more than twice his seriousness.

Perhaps one of the most curious attributes of acting is the inability of the actor to control his own projections. Just as an author will find a character running away with him, so will an actor find his characters taking to life wilfully, on their own account. Let any well-trained actor come on to the stage and, with his mind fixed on vacancy, utter half-a-dozen lines. We shall immediately find the words and the character uttering them pregnant with a world of meaning. We shall find that the words have, of their own accord, started a train of thought in our brain over which the actor has had scant influence or none. It is not the mind of the player but his physical presentiment which carries over to the spectator. It takes a very bad actor indeed to prevent an audience from eking him out ; and perhaps we may say that the very good actor is the actor who can satisfy an intellectual audience and think of his supper at the same time. A great part of the actor's art consists in letting the spectator do the thinking. Even should the actor make the mistake of trying to do all the thinking for himself, he has no guarantee that the spectator will not prefer his own train of thought. It follows that with anything like a capable critic the actor is always in danger of the cleverest misinterpretation.

A good many years ago one of our most scholarly actors was in the habit of flouting the box-office with occasional performances of King Richard the Second. This actor's interpretation of the sickly and sentimental king was one day discovered by a famous dramatic critic, who proceeded to weave round it a most beautiful and penetrative piece of criticism. After a wonderfully fine definition of what makes the true artist—so fine that it is surely the best ever written—the critic proceeded to nail his definition to Shakespeare's Richard and, as he supposed, to the actor's also. In this wonderful impersonation, fitting Shakespeare's Richard and the player's own talent like a glove, there was just one wrinkle from which not even the subtlest of critics, though he noted it duly, could have been expected to deduce a complete misfit. Let me quote the criticism :

In Richard every other feeling is mastered, except at a few passing moments, by a passion of interest in the exercise of his gift of exquisite responsiveness to the appeal made to his artistic sensibility by whatever life throws for the moment in his way. Lamb said it was worth while to have been cheated of the legacy so as not to miss " the idea of " the rogue who did it. That, on a little scale, is the kind of

28

The Actor as Charlatan

æsthetic disinterestedness which in Shakespeare's Richard, rightly presented by Mr. Benson, passes all bounds. The "idea of" a king's fall, the "idea of" a wife and husband torn apart, the "idea of" a very crucifixion of indignities—as each new idea comes he revels in his own warmed and lighted apprehension of it as freely as in his apprehension of the majesty and mystery of the idea of a kingship by divine right. He runs out to meet the thought of a lower fall or a new shame as a man might go to his door to see a sunset or a storm. It has been called the aim of artistic culture to witness things with appropriate emotions. That is this Richard's aim. Good news or bad news, the first thing with him is to put himself in the right vein for getting the fullest and most poignant sense of its contents. Is ruin the word—his mind runs to steep itself in relevant pathos with which in turn to saturate the object put before it ; he will "talk of graves and epitaphs," "talk of wills," "tell sad stories of the death of kings." Once in the vein, he rejoices like a good artist who has caught the spirit of his subject. The very sense of the loss of hope becomes "that sweet way I was in to despair." To his wife at their last meeting he bequeaths, as one imaginative writer might bequeath to another some treasure of possibilities of tragic effect, "the lamentable tale of me."

To this intoxicating sense of the beauty or poignancy of what is next him he joins the true passion of concern for its perfect expression. At the height of that preoccupation enmities, fears, mortifications, the very presence of onlookers are as if they were not. At the climax of the agony of the abdication scene Shakespeare, with a magnificent boldness of truth, makes the artist's mind, in travail with the lovely poetical figure of the mirror, snatch at the possibility of help at the birth of the beautiful thing, even from the bitterest enemy,—

> Say that again ;
> The shadow of my sorrow ; ha, let's see.

Buzz, Buzz !

And nothing in Mr. Benson's performance was finer than the king's air, during the mirror soliloquy, as of a man going about his mind's engrossing business in a solitude of its own making. He gave their full value, again, to all those passages, so enigmatic, if not ludicrous, to strictly prosaic minds, in which Richard's craving for finished expression issues in a joining of words with figurative action to point and eke them out; as where he gives away the crown in the simile of the well, inviting his enemy, with the same artistic neutrality as in the passage of the mirror, to collaborate manually in an effort to give perfect expression to the situation. With Aumerle Richard is full of these little symbolic inventions, turning them over lovingly as a writer fondles a phrase that tells. "Would not this ill do well," he says of one of them, like a poet showing a threnody to a friend.

There was just one point—perhaps it was a mere slip— at which Mr. Benson seemed to us to fail. In the beginning of the scene at Pomfret what one may call the artistic heroism of this man, so craven in everything but art, reaches its climax. Ruined, weary, with death waiting in the next room, he is shown still toiling at the attainment of a perfect, because perfectly expressed, apprehension of such flat dregs as are left him of life, still following passionately on the old quest of the ideal word, the unique image, the one perfect way of saying the one thing.

> I cannot do it ; yet I'll hammer it out.

Everybody knows that cry of the artist wrestling with the angel in the dark for the word it will not give, of Balzac " plying the pick for dear life, like an entombed miner," of our own Stevenson, of Flaubert " sick, irritated, the prey a thousand times a day of cruel pain," but " continuing my labour like a true working man, who, with sleeves turned up, in the sweat of his brow, beats away at his anvil, whether it rain or blow, hail or thunder." That " yet I'll hammer it

30

The Actor as Charlatan

out " is the gem of the whole passage, yet on Saturday Mr. Benson, by some strange mischance, left the words clean out. He made amends with a beautiful little piece of insight at the close, where, after the lines—

> Mount, mount, my soul ! Thy seat is up on high,
> Whilst my gross flesh sinks downward, here to die,

uttered much as any other man might utter them under the first shock of the imminence of death, he half rises from the ground with a brightened face and repeats the two last words with a sudden return of animation and interest, the eager spirit leaping up, with a last flicker before it goes quite out, to seize on this new " idea of " the death of the body. Greater love of art could no man have than this, and, if we understood him rightly, it was a brilliant thought of Mr. Benson's to end on such a note. But indeed the whole performance, but for the slip we have mentioned, was brilliant in its equal grasp of the two sides of the character, the one which everybody sees well enough and the one which nearly everybody seems to shun seeing, and in the value which it rendered to the almost continuous flow of genuine and magnificent poetry from Richard, to the descant on mortality in kings, for instance, and the exquisite greeting to English soil and the gorgeous rhetoric of the speeches on divine right in kings.

The careful reader will have noted the fourfold insistence of the critic on his own misgivings—" if we understood him rightly," " by some strange mischance," and twice the reference to a possible slip. Hear now the sequel.

With this wonderful piece of criticism in my ears, and being not more than twenty at the time, I went to see the King Richard the Second of Mr. Benson, as he then was. Trembling with excite-

31

Buzz, Buzz !

ment, I persisted with door-keepers until, after the fourth act, they let me into Richard's presence. To whom I reeled off as much as I could remember of the famous criticism, winding up with the eager question as to whether the omission of the significant line was accidental or not. Mr. Benson heard me out with the greatest politeness, and then proceeded to teach me my first lesson in a proper understanding of the actor as conscious visionary and subconscious charlatan. Mr. Benson said it had never occurred to him to think of the King in the wonderful light in which my critical friend presented him. *He had never thought of the unhappy monarch in any æsthetic or self-conscious connection whatever.* He had never regarded him as a *poseur*. Rather had he viewed him . . . I forget now in exactly what light Mr. Benson professed to view his own creation ; there was, if I remember rightly, some question of Gibbon and the Decline and Fall. I was too much overwhelmed to grasp any alternative theory. In reply to my further question as to the omission of the famous line, the actor confessed that he did not attach importance to these particular words, and that he left them out intentionally !

I went back to my seat and had a practical verification of this non-attaching of importance to what the finest of critics had proclaimed to be the essential line. The words were again omitted. Then, either to make amends, or for sheer plaguing's sake, Mr. Benson recovered the missing line and

The Actor as Charlatan

pitchforked it gratuitously and even wittily into the text at a place where the insertion did not make too great a hash of the sense.

> *K. Rich.* I have been studying how I may compare
> This prison where I live unto the world :
> And for because the world is populous,
> And here is not a creature but myself,
> I cannot do it ; *yet I'll hammer it out,*
> My brain I'll prove the female to my soul ;
> My soul the father : etc. etc.

is the passage in which occurred Mr. Benson's sin of omission. The honours of reparation were given to the passage :

> Music do I hear?
> Ha, ha ! keep time. How sour sweet music is
> When time is broke and no proportion kept !
> *Yet I'll hammer it out.*
> So is it in the music of men's lives.

And as I went home that night I made up my mind once and for all that, pull devil, pull baker, the critic has as much right to his interpretation as the actor, and that the true Richard of Mr. Benson, whatever the actor might declare to the contrary, was to be found in a certain piece of criticism first printed in *The Manchester Guardian* on December 4, 1899, over the initials C. E. M., and republished in that remarkable little volume, *The Manchester Stage, 1880-1900.*[1]

[1] It should not be necessary to state that my intention is *not* to brand as charlatans the actors alluded to above. One of them, Sir F. R. Benson, I consider, for reasons given elsewhere, the finest living English actor. The point is that God has given the actor one face, as Hamlet pointed out long ago, that it is his profession to make himself another, and the privilege of the spectator to imagine a third. The charlatanism, if any, is to be looked for in the fact that these masks can be so superimposed, and not in the actor who is following his legitimate trade.

The Actor as Artist

ACTORS there are who plead that they would be glad enough be artists if the public would only let them. Again one has to quote Berlioz, who, writing somewhere of Madame Sontag, says that she was the only singer of his day who would risk her reputation by singing *piano*. Berlioz goes on to declare that a *piano*, a *pianissimo* even, can be got for the asking out of an orchestra a hundred strong or a choir double the number (an orchestra, like any other composite body, has neither individual soul to save nor individual body to be done violence to), but that from the *diva*, be she clever or unskilful, intelligent or stupid, human or divine, no *piano* is obtainable by flattery or threat, cajolery or whiplash. That Berlioz was right in his time those will concede who realise how rare, even to-day, in the speaking theatre, is the actor who will subordinate himself, who will allow that his art can have its *diminuendos* as well as its *crescendos*. " Vous avez bien fait de venir m'entendre ce soir," exclaimed a great French actress after a particularly fine performance, " Dieu même me soufflait." A *forfanterie* with the obvious implication that on occasion the divine fire might be lacking.

I remember a performance of Daudet's *l'Arlésienne* given during the war in the famous Roman arena of Arles. It was a blazing hot day even for Provence, and the sun veering round the corner of the rickety awning must have been terribly trying to the courage of the actors and to their tempers,

The Actor as Artist

which showed signs of wear as the afternoon drew to evening. It was a scratch cast headed by the one-time celebrated Aimée Tessandier,[1] and containing among others a robustious veteran whom one seemed to have been applauding in secondary rôles for half a lifetime, a tepid little goose and an enthusiastic *jeune premier* whose name I forget, but who struck me as being about the best in that line.

[1] An admirable actress if never quite of the highest order. Her book of recollections is full of good things. The artist relates her past with an amazing frankness, beginning with the days when as a child she was forced to pick up dung on the high-roads, and making no secret of her years of notoriety as a beauty. As an example of her wit and sincerity we may instance her own description of her efforts to acquire an American accent for the part of Julia Waker in Pailleron's *L'Age ingrat*.

"Me jeter à l'eau, cela veut dire que je vais essayer l'accent. J'essaie. Ça ne vient pas. Je n'ai pas de dispositions, et pourtant je fais de mon mieux ; je cours les bars, je commande des *sodas*, *du whisky*, du *pale-ale*, j'attrape des crampes d'estomac ; je pénètre dans tous les magasins britanniques ; je me ruine en objets à dénominations anglaises,—je dus récemment me débarrasser d'un stock important de *waterproofs* acquis à cette époque,—on me rencontre sur tous les champs de courses, dans des écuries, je fréquente des *jockeys*, des *lads*, est-ce que je sais ? Je me fais présenter un nombre invraisemblable de *misses* et de *mistress*, j'emploie des journées entières à articuler *goddam, thank you, how do you do, Washington, kiss me, cow-boy, good-bye, good-night*—et cela sans prendre l'accent. Si des Américaines passent dans la rue, je me précipite, je les suis de près, je bois leurs paroles, et même, les jours de grande énergie, j'interviens dans leurs conversations. Mes amis craignent qu'à force de bonnes intentions, je ne me fasse remarquer."

("In for a penny in for a pound, which means that I am going to have a try at the accent. My first efforts meet with no success. I am no hand at it, and yet I do my very best. "I visit bars, I order *whisky-and-sodas* and *pale ale* ; I get stomach-ache ; I go into all the English shops ; I ruin myself in articles with English names—it is only recently that I got rid of a huge stock of *waterproofs* bought at this period—I go to all the races, I am to be found in the stables, in the company of *jockeys*, *lads*, or whatever you call them. I arrange for an incredible number of *Misses* and *Mistresses* to be presented to me ; I spend whole days in pronouncing *Goddam, thank you, how do you do, Washington, kiss me, cow-boy, good-bye, good-night,*—and still I can't manage the accent. When I pass American women in the street I quicken my step, follow close behind, and drink in their words. When I am in a really energetic mood I mix myself up in their conversation. My friends are afraid that through excess of zeal I shall attract too much attention.")

35

Buzz, Buzz !

The scenery was of the barest description. A crazy door in the back wall would swing open now and again to reveal the Mère Renaud, a stout, red-faced woman, indulging stertorously in an after-dinner nap prior to her exquisite scene with her septuagenarian lover — the old stager before mentioned, who seemed a deal more intent on catching the *rapide* back to Paris than on the belated endearments of his antique mistress. A local band of enthusiasts was more than persistent in its endeavours to get the better of Bizet's immortal little suite—that perfect justification of incidental music. There were numerous stage waits ; the Arlesian Don José, who in the play could not be got to listen to the wooings of his Micaela, could be heard prompting her with her own proper blandishments. In the front row of the so-called balcony—the first tier of the old arena—an enormous and disconcerting negro shone and basked, and rolled under his red fez the yellows of his bilious eyes. Boys whooped and skylarked, clambering over the tiers, leaping from arch to arch, and chasing one another up and down the stone stairways. Seagulls from the Mediterranean — *mouettes* the peasant of the Midi calls them—wheeled and complained high in the blue, and once a *grand-duc* on some majestic journey paused for a contemptuous glance at the mimic scene.

It was a combination to dismay a lesser genius than Tessandier's, but this fine artist knew how to triumph over the accident of a setting and the

absurdities of the Provençal stage. Up to the end
of the fourth act the old lady had given a wonderful
performance, full of vigour and authority, if something lacking in charm. So would Geneviève
Ward have played Rose Mamaï, one thought, with
a stern, unbending, almost feline quality of motherhood. But when the players came on for the fifth
act, it could be seen that the old lady had gone to
pieces. I have said that the staging was entirely
inadequate. Those who have seen *l'Arlésienne*
will remember the formidable staircase of the last
act down which it is the tradition for the mother
to *dégringoler*. It was whispered amongst the
audience that the properties of the Arena *did not
contain a staircase.* Just as well, one thought, since
the old lady would be spared the physical effort.
So we applauded respectfully, since the earlier acts
had been magnificent, and wended our way soberly
home.

I made a little detour in order to visit the ruins
of the Greek Theatre on the hill, so that when I
arrived at the hotel the artists had preceded me.
In the *salon* I found a little, old, withered, shrunken
figure. It was Tessandier, rocking herself to and
fro, crying with rage. I attempted some formal
complimenting, which was interrupted by a storm
of protest and the unhooding of the old lady's
angry eyes, the eyes of a vulture, they seemed to me.

"Non, Monsieur, ce n'était pas ça ! Au contraire, j'ai très mal joué. C'était vraiment trop
fort. On m'avait promis le nécessaire, et vous

37

Buzz, Buzz !

avez vu comme ces messieurs savent tenir leur
parole. Je n'avais même pas l'escalier pour le
cinqième acte ! C'était indigne, c'était lâche. Un
moment j'eus l'idée de quitter la scène et de retourner
à Paris, car je prévoyais que le dernier acte serait
forcément râté, et que je manquerais mon effet.
Ainsi je ne fus plus maîtresse de moi-même, et j'ai
très mal joué ! " [1]

Then in a paroxysm of self-reproach : " Il m'a
fallu manquer mon effet. J'ai dû jouer au-dessous
de mes forces ! " [2]

To my fumbling consolation that one cannot
always be at one's best, the actress replied with
dignity : " A mon âge, Monsieur, je n'ai pas. le
droit de jouer au-dessous de mes forces ! " [3]

At her age ! There lay the sting of the reproach.
One realised that to this artist it was a pitiful thing
to quit the scene on an anti-climax. At her age !
The chance that a great career might close on a
fiasco was more than she could bear.

I do not know a better example of the actor as
artist.

[1] " No, Monsieur, it was not well played ! On the contrary, I acted very
badly. But then it was really too annoying. The management promised me
everything I required, and you see how they kept their word. There was not
even the staircase for the fifth act. It was disgraceful, dishonourable. At one
moment I thought of abandoning the performance and going straight back to
Paris, for I foresaw that the last act could only be a fiasco, and that my last
scene must be spoiled. I could not regain control of myself, with the result
that I played very badly."

[2] " I could do nothing to prevent my scene from being spoiled. I was forced
to play below my best."

[3] " At my age, Monsieur, I cannot allow myself to play below my best."

Boiled Leg of Mutton

A THEATRICAL "swarry" in the days of our grand-fathers consisted in a formal *pièce de résistance*, by which one meant the acting and the usual trimmings, to wit, the fashionable crowd, the lights, the chatter, the music, and the play. In these latter days what was once the well-defined if rule-of-thumb business of stage-managing has passed into the hands of a so-called " producer " or " Art Director "—this grotesque nomenclature has been seen on an actual theatre programme—with the result that an evening at the play is become a phantasmagoria of all the arts, a consummation which, under the guise of reinforcing the player, would appear to the plain man to conduce to his belittlement and ultimate extinction. Now your new-fangled Art Director can, of course, put up a wonderful case for himself on paper. Whoever heard, he will say, of the human face being lit up from the cellar instead of by the divine light of heaven ? Which naturalistic and pietistic argument is adduced to cover the abolition of footlights and the introduction of a system of top-lighting aided by batteries of efful-gence converging on the player from such part of the vault of heaven as may be represented by the dress-circle. It is here to be noted that your Art Director, who is all for the fine shades in the thousand and one irrelevancies which he would superimpose upon the stage, has never the ghost of a glimmering of a feeling *for the theatre* in the old-fashioned meaning of the phrase. It

39

Buzz, Buzz !

is worth while clearing this up before we go any further.

All stage plays are pictures of a world removed from the spectator, cut off from and presented to his consciousness by the gilt and moulding of the proscenium. It is vital to the art of the actor that he shall *keep his frame*, and that there shall be no point of contact between him and the spectator. (This isolation and setting back of the player is admirably insisted upon by the use of a gauze for the production of fairy plays.) The actor cannot commit a greater fault than to emerge beyond his proper plane ; a hair's-breadth advance into the breathing world is utter annihilation. No play-goer imbued with the rightful and legitimate contempt for the monkeyings of Grand Opera can ever have witnessed without the most intense and savage satisfaction the destruction of the last vestiges of verisimilitude achieved by these antics [1] when, reeking with garlic and macaroni, they leave their preposterous kingdom to sway and bawl in the half-light over the prompter's box. Equally disastrous to illusion is the contact established between player and spectator by the beams of light connecting the front of the house with the stage.

Equally disastrous, by inversion, the mania for regarding footlights as a fourth wall. This stretching of legs to imaginary fireplaces audiencewards,

---

[1] In the Shakespearean sense, "And there the antick sits." For the effectiveness of this outburst of temper I presume my tenors and baritones to be of the Italian variety which hails from Marseilles.

Boiled Leg of Mutton

that warming of hands over the well of the orchestra at the beaming stove which is the countenance of the gratified conductor, the very insistence on the absence of an audience serves only to reinforce in the consciousness of that audience the feeling that they are but spectators and that the thing they are looking at is but a play. Whereas the whole virtue of the frame and the picture, the aloofness and the setting-back is the illusion produced in the spectator that he has happened upon life. Those doubting Thomases among my readers who are still unconvinced should have sat with me in the front row of stalls at the Savoy Theatre, amazed out of all apprehension of the play by a gigantic floorcloth of sea-green which, whilst pretending to be the carpet of a doctor's consulting-room, overflowed from stage to auditorium, swamped the orchestra, and splashed terrifyingly about our feet.

" Now, then, gentlemen," this playwright of the consulting-room seemed to be saying, " I am to tell you that I am very much one of yourselves, and that these actors of mine are very much of the same stuff as yourselves also. There is nothing to be alarmed at. I am just going to drag all your family skeletons out of their cupboards and let you and my actors have a nice little confidential chat about them. Are we all comfortable ? Quite sure ? No barriers between us ? Then let the play begin."

With the result that I came out of the theatre feeling as though I had spent the afternoon in the

Buzz, Buzz !

dissecting-room at Guy's. Whereas when, later on, I saw the same play in a stuffy little provincial theatre, all red velvet curtains and obvious footlights, I felt that it was as to four-fifths of it, one of the most delightful, witty, ironical, and moving representations of real life I had ever witnessed.

Then we come to the sprightly and symbolistic vein of production, in which your Art Director can be seen tacking on to the chins of Shakespeare's fairy creatures beards of tin-foil, of which both the amusingness and the symbolism have always escaped me. Or—and this is the most mischievous —your Art Director will have it that the scenery is the thing. I shall always hold the spirit of motherhood to be capable of no greater sacrifice than that shown by Miss Ellen Terry [1] when she delivered her Beatrice to the scenic mercies of Mr. Gordon Craig. Two reasons may be assigned for Miss Terry's triumph : either she is so great an actress that no possible or conceivable—by which I mean impossible and inconceivable— setting can daunt her, or Mr. Craig tempered his genius with filial consideration.

I shall attempt to deal later with the argument that the intention of these new-fangled contrivers is to brace the actor and not to do battle with him. For the moment I will contend that it is possible to arrange a setting—let me be frank and say that

[1] This devotion of Miss Ellen Terry's reminds one of the French story of the mother's bleeding heart which, being conveyed as a son's offering to his mistress, exclaimed as the boy stumbled : " *T'es-tu fait mal, mon fils ?* " (" Are you hurt, my son ? ")

Boiled Leg of Mutton

Mr. Craig has actually arranged such settings, which by themselves make up so tremendous a sea of emotion that no actor could hope to live in it. Take the model of the staircase down which Macbeth is to come half in panic, half in awe, finger on lip, knees giving, heart quaking, his whole soul sagging, his speech and his lady's cut into little steps—a very staircase of fear :

> *Macb.* I have done the deed. Didst thou not hear a noise ?
> *Lady M.* I heard the owl scream and the crickets cry.
> Did not you speak ?
> *Macb.*   When ?
> *Lady M.*   Now.
> *Macb.*   As I descended ?
> *Lady M.* Ay.
> *Macb.* Hark !
> Who lies i' the second chamber ?
> *Lady M.*   Donalbain.

I remember thinking when I saw the model that whereas an actor has all his work cut out to parry comparison with the staircase of words in the printed book, he would have no chance at all against the terror of this imaginative piece of cardboard. For the whole case against Mr. Craig lies in the fact that he has done his work too magnificently. His art is not supplementary, but complete in itself, and demands prime recognition. We feel that in such a setting the actor is a trespasser.

The whole case for the modern Art Director rests on his contention that the actor is the representative of a single art, whereas a theatrical performance should be a compendium of many. And

43

Buzz, Buzz !

like all people with a poor case, he is not to be restrained from pushing analogy to its furthest limits. A great picture, he will say, may make as many simultaneous appeals as it likes. It may attract by the quality of its design, by the lure of its colour, by telling a good story about Venus or Oliver Cromwell or the Young Man who fed upon Husks, by being good to the touch. Why should not the theatre be entitled to as manifold an appeal as a picture ? That the theatre *is* a picture he will maintain stoutly. And he will go on to claim for the theatre not that quality of remoteness, of being gathered into a frame, which was the basis of my own pictorial contention, but also all the other attributes to be looked for in a picture. Why should not the theatre, he will say, attract by design, colour, story, by being good to handle ?

We come here, I think, to the modern danger threatening the whole art of the actor. I have always believed that the actor's needs could be limited to a couple of boards to stand him on, a back-cloth to set him against, and a light to see him by, were it not that bare boards and plain back-cloths are, in their way, as abnormal and disturbing as the excesses of over-staging. In this search for the unremarkable there is a good deal to be said for the undistinguished sets of the touring company of commerce. One seems to have seen all of Sir F. R. Benson's productions and a great many of Sir Herbert Tree's with the strange experience that whereas one remembers

44

everything of the acting in the former instance and little or nothing in the latter, the scenery in both cases has left no impression whatever. Riot and lavishness amounting to confusion are akin to meagreness in that they make equally little impression on the mind. Curiously enough, vulgarity of setting does less damage to the actor than the exquisite and the strange. Tawdriness merely embarrasses him ; it is the competitive exquisite which annihilates him.

I have always believed, and must believe still, that there is no corner of the mind the supreme actor cannot fill. To demand more than acting from the theatre is to argue a lukewarmness about the art like that of the half-hearted *gourmet* who should demand a wit to listen to, music to be conscious of, and a crowd of other diners to distract him. It may be argued that in these circumstances the eating-house is a pleasanter place, or even that something short of the highest quality of food can be put up with. This is not altogether to be denied any more than I will deny that, with indifferent acting, the theatre may be a pleasanter place for having a Craig to look at and a Debussy to listen to. But just as your *gourmet*, confronted with a royal dish, will stop eyes and ears and all other avenues of sense save the palate alone, so will the spectator, faced with a royal actor, ask nothing of scene-painter and electrician, wardrobe-director and composer of soft music. He will be satisfied with acting alone.

Buzz, Buzz !

In the rare case of your Art Director being a good tactician, he will try to get you to meet him on the lower ground that he is first and foremost a practical man ; that he has to take things as he finds them ; that we live in a world where there is not always a royal actor on hand ; and that certainly there will never be enough of the species to go round. He will argue that beautiful scenery may help moderate acting ; that it won't do any harm ; that it can't be as bad as bad scenery ; that it must increase the sum of enjoyment. Well, this is a reasonable position not easy to assail. But it is rare that so modest a claim is put forward by your Art Director, who will insist upon being sponge and bottle-holder to the royal actor as well as to the mediocre. Against which it is to be maintained that the human mind is incapable of registering more than one intense impression at a time. To put it simply, if you feel acting fully you have no emotion to spare for scenery, and *vice versa*.[1] Hence it follows that scenery which attracts attention to itself must necessarily subtract from the attention which it is possible to give to the actor.

This exaltation of the producer above the actor

[1] I suppose every playgoer has been moved to the utmost of his being by the Marguerite Gauthier of Sarah Bernhardt. If this be ruled out as mere pathetical debauchery, let me make confession of being moved to the top of any possible æsthetic bent of mine by her Pelléas. The *décor* on this occasion was some tawdry rubbish which had done duty for the provincial pantomime of " Red Riding Hood," and there was the usual provincial orchestra. Nevertheless, I maintain that the sum of pleasure would not have been increased if the Heavenly Choir had been in attendance to blow on silver trumpets the most ravishing strains of a Debussy, or if the shades of Claude, Poussin, and Corot had returned to earth to take turns with the scene-painter's brush.

Boiled Leg of Mutton

I regard as the first step on the road to the latter's total demolition. For demolition it is going to be. Hear Mr. Arthur Symons :

> After seeing a ballet, a farce, and the fragment of an opera performed by the marionettes at the Costanzi Theatre in Rome, I am inclined to ask myself why we require the intervention of any less perfect medium between the meaning of a piece, as the author conceived it, and that other meaning which it derives from our reception of it. The living actor, even when he condescends to subordinate himself to the requirements of pantomime, has always what he is proud to call his temperament; in other words, so much personal caprice, which for the most part means wilful misunderstanding; and in seeing his acting you have to consider this intrusive little personality of his as well as the author's. The marionette may be relied upon. He will respond to an indication without reserve or revolt; an error on his part (we are all human) will certainly be the fault of the author; he can be trained to perfection. As he is painted, so will he smile; as the wires lift or lower his hands, so will his gestures be; and he will dance when his legs are set in motion.

Never was question so beautifully begged ; so exquisite indeed is the whole essay that it would be a crime against æsthetics to dash it with argument. One phrase alone sticks in our throats—*the intrusive little personality of the actor*. Here we get to the damnable root of the matter. To me the theatre has always meant *the actor*, though it be Shakespeare that he plays at. True that I feel guilty of an infidelity to the Falstaff of Shakespeare whenever I take to marvelling at some mountain of bolster or whole merchant's venture of horsehair pretending

47

to be that piece of sweet beef. But it is unfaithfulness at one remove only, and though I be forced to pardon the intrusion on my Shakespeare of the " little personality " of the actor, I will be party to no further infidelities.

It is time to deal with the argument that the producer comes to reinforce the actor and not to overwhelm him. Any such argument must always be on the lines of the poet's declaration as to the marriage of perfect music and perfect words, which anybody but a poet would know to be impossible. Perfect words and perfect music mean words and music so perfectly charged with emotion of their own kind and so perfectly expressed in their own way that no addition of emotion is possible.[1] You may compare them to two perfectly full glasses, neither of which can by any possible sleight of hand be emptied into the other. The result of any such attempt must necessarily be a spill. The result of setting perfect words to perfect music is that of two fine things one must inevitably be spilled or destroyed. There is bound to be a surrender, and it almost always happens that it is the words which give way.

[1] That music will always triumph over words is proved by the fact that the most exquisite operas of Mozart and Weber have achieved immortality in the face of perfectly lunatic libretti ; by the fact that we are capable of being ravished to the top of our bent by *arias* in unknown lingos. (It is true that there are a certain number of literary and non-musical Germans who rave over the *Lieder* of Schubert because the words happen to be by Goethe. To the musician who is non-literary the words are as nothing. To the average individual with a fair sense of both arts the words are little better than nothing.) By the fact, too, that whereas the average concert-goer will hum you Elgar's themes for *Gerontius*, he will not be able to quote a line of Newman's book.

Boiled Leg of Mutton

I may perhaps be permitted to give a school-boy illustration—that song of Ariel's which Shakespeare in gentle modesty offered to the music-makers of his time :

> Full fathom five thy father lies ;
> Of his bones are coral made ;
> Those are pearls that were his eyes :
> Nothing of him that doth fade
> But doth suffer a sea-change
> Into something rich and strange.
> Sea-nymphs hourly ring his knell :
> (*Burden*) : ding-dong.
> Hark ! now I hear them,—ding-dong, bell.

It is not that the tapestried majestical of this verse is beyond the powers of, say, the Brahms who wrote the *Four Serious Songs*, but that the more wonderful the musical setting, the more inevitable the translation into another atmosphere. Nothing of Shakespeare's verse but must inevitably fade into the web woven by the musician. It is probable that to every reader of Shakespeare these words bring a slightly different atmosphere. In me they conjure up visions of mother-of-pearl cathedrals rising from ghostly seas, to the pealing of sunken bells and the wan wash of tides. Perhaps the long " a's " in *made, fade, change, strange* are responsible for this. Now let your musician come along.

In other words, the musical appeal is more direct than the literary. Besides, does not the one actually drown the other ? A great French actress used to tell her pupils that the *sound* of verse is the first, if not the only consideration. "If people want to know what a poem is about," she would say, "they can always ask to have it recited a second time."

49

Buzz, Buzz !

Let him set the words never so subtly, never so gloriously, *he can never reproduce the long "a's."* At best he can but attain a different ghostliness and another vision.

As the unnecessary, meaningless, and harmful tinkle—which is all that even perfect music may be when superimposed upon perfect words—so the would-be elucidatory illustrations to Shakespeare. Says Lamb: " I rather prefer the common editions of Roe and Tonson, without notes and with *plates*, which, being so execrably bad, serve as maps or modest remembrancers to the text ; and, without pretending to any supposable emulation with it, are so much better than the Shakespeare gallery *engravings*, which *did*."

The thing is cumulative. As the musician and the illustrator, so the scene - painter, decorator, producer, Art Director. Can we imagine Mr. Craig or any other artist being satisfied with a theory of staging which should consider his wonderful arrangements as just so many maps or modest remembrancers to a text ? Go to ! As well be a mere translator ! Mr. Craig and his kind are artists as well as Shakespeare ; the rôle of understudy is not for them. When we listen to Shakespeare's verse we are to feel in terms of Shakespeare ; when we look at Mr. Craig's settings we are to feel in terms of Mr. Craig. And never the twain shall interpret one another, though you put them on the stage together and with every pretence of mutual support.

Boiled Leg of Mutton

One section of the drama for actors I am prepared to hand over to the Art Director, and that is certain of the comedies of Shakespeare. Let happen what will to the fairy scenes of *A Midsummer Night's Dream*, *Love's Labour's Lost*, and *The Tempest*. Let the decorative worst befall the romantical parts of *Twelfth Night* and *The Winter's Tale*, in the *action* of which I can imagine no sane person taking interest, and which the Art Director has my full leave to turn if he like into a ballet.[1] But hands off *As You Like It* and *The Merchant of Venice*, *Measure for Measure*, and *Much Ado*. Hands off the human interludes in the fairy comedies. Hands off Bottom, Snug, and Snout. Hands off Starveling and Flute. Hands off Sir Andrew Aguecheek and old Sir Toby. Hands off Portia and Isabella (though she was a prig), Beatrice and Rosalind. How can a miserable horde of Art Directors hope to succeed where even that most exquisite and illustrious of critics, Théophile Gautier, failed so miserably? Like him, they would turn the gossamer and dew of *As You Like It* into the cotton-wool of *Comme il vous plaira*. The truth of the matter would seem to be that whereas acting is a great art and play-writing a great art also, there is no *art of the theatre* which combines the two, except it be the Ballet. There the movements of the dancers are arranged to be in harmony with and to complete the design of the scene, putting,

---

[1] The poetry of these plays is the affair of the study. I am inclined to think that Shakespeare put all the scenery he cared about into his lines.

Buzz, Buzz !

as it were, an outline round the music. In ballet the arts are complementary and not supplementary, that is to say, the one is not more important than the other. It may even be that the stage as a medium for pure acting is less deserving of consideration now that the poets leave it severely alone ; that it degrades itself in its present-day allegiance to what a middling wit has described as " stuffy Ibsenism with its aroma of yesterday's cold mutton," the social comedies of Mayfair and the touring " London Success." The art of ballet being unknown, or at least non-existent in this country, it follows that the only medium making appeal alike to eye and ear and intelligence is *Revue*. *Revue* our only art of the theatre ! Lame, logical, impotent, absurd conclusion. A true conclusion however, since in *revue* the manifold appeal, so dear to the heart of the Art Director, is at least made, though it be made execrably. Which reminds me of the distinction once drawn between the wives of two famous actor-managers—Madame X declared no actress at all, Mistress Z allowed an actress, but a very bad one.

To sum up. Hands off, Messieurs the Art Directors, such great plays as we have and such great players as the gods may send us ! Betake yourselves over the way to the palaces of *Revue*. There you will find some good comic acting, plenty of pretty ladies with reputations for pearls if for nothing else, lithe and agreeable dancers, and an audience indifferent as to whether they go to the

Boiled Leg of Mutton

footlights or the footlights come to them. In such a *milieu* you may produce and art-direct as you will. There production and plenty of it is the thing. You may produce beautifully, wistfully, wilfully even. There will be none to say you nay.[1]

---

[1] It may be urged that the foregoing resembles the speech of the Parliamentary duffer, inasmuch as that part of it which is new is not true, and that part which is true is not new. It is, however, an agreeable if humiliating experience to find that some startling and original discovery has all along been part and parcel of the eternal verities. I retain my argument, therefore, whilst giving chapter and verse of an earlier statement unknown to me until after the manuscript of the present book had left my hands. In Rousseau's *Dictionnaire de Musique*, compiled in 1750 and printed at Geneva in 1781, the reader will find the following passage under the word *Opéra* :

"Mais on ne peut marcher long-tems dans la route du bon goût sans monter ou descendre, & la perfection est un point où il est difficile de se maintenir. Après avoir essayé & senti ses forces, la Musique en état de marcher seule commence à dédaigner la Poésie qu'elle doit accompagner, & croit en valoir mieux en tirant d'elle-même les beautés qu'elle partageoit avec sa compagne. Elle se propose encore, il est vrai, de rendre les idées & les sentimens du Poète ; mais elle prend, en quelque sorte, un autre langage, & quoique l'objet soit le même, le Poète & le Musicien trop séparés dans leur travail en offrent à la fois deux images ressemblantes, mais distinctes, qui se nuisent mutuellement. L'esprit forcé de se partager choisit, & se fixe à une image plutôt qu'à l'autre. Alors le Musicien, s'il a plus d'art que le Poète, l'efface & le fait oublier ; l'Acteur voyant que le Spectateur sacrifie les paroles à la Musique, sacrifie à son tour le Geste & l'Action théâtrale au Chant & au brillant de la voix ; ce qui fait tout-à-fait oublier la Pièce, & change le Spectacle en un véritable Concert. Que si l'avantage au contraire se trouve du côté du Poète, la Musique à son tour deviendra presque indifférente, & le Spectateur trompé par le bruit pourra prendre le change au point d'attribuer à un mauvais Musicien le mérite d'un excellent Poète, & de croire admirer des chef-d'œuvres d'Harmonie en admirant des poèmes bien composés."

("One cannot keep the highway of good taste for long together without some rise and fall, and there is difficulty in remaining at the point of perfection. After making trial of her strength and finding herself able to walk alone, the Art of Music came to look scornfully upon the Art of Poetry with whom she had borne company, and to seek her own advantage in relying upon herself alone for those beauties which she had formerly shared. While still proposing to render the ideas and sentiments of the Poet, she created a new language, so that the Poet and Musician, though sharing the same object, went to work in different ways. By this means they produced two distinct images which, for all their resemblance,

53

Buzz, Buzz !

were harmful to each other. The mind, divided against itself, was forced to make a choice and to set one image above another. In the case in which the Musician was the greater artist it followed that he effaced and eclipsed the Poet ; the Actor, conscious of the Spectator's preference of words to Music, sacrificed in his turn Action and Gesture to the Art of Singing and the Beauty of the Voice. Of this the result was the abandonment of the Play and the usurpation of Drama by the Concert. When the Poet was master he relegated Music to the background, whereupon the Spectator's judgment, confused by the din, was led into according to a bad Musician the meed of a good Poet, and even into attributing to a masterpiece of Harmony the delight due to an admirable Poem.")

In other words, the Spectator cannot applaud two masters. Add the scene-painter, and still less do I perceive how he is going to pay tribute to three.

The Pros and Cons

It would perhaps be an exaggeration to say that the most famous scenes in the *Comédie Humaine* of Balzac take place in the boxes at the Opera or in the *foyer* at the Italiens. I do not, in point of fact, remember any particular occasion on which these actors from the Faubourg St. Germain borrowed their setting from the corridors and staircases of their theatres except the famous scene between Beatrix and Calyste. But there prevails throughout Balzac the note that the theatre is the meeting-place proper to the passions. Within its walls dramas other than the ostensible fictions of the stage are in rehearsal, could you get wind of them; the world at its best and its seamiest is agog with business of its own. There are those in the audience, you feel, who, unmoved by the painted peril of the scene, cast from time to time a nervous glance over their shoulders. . . .

It was not without intent that the Baron de Louvenjoul, in his attempt to carry the lives of the characters of the *Comédie* a step further, assembled them in stalls and boxes. To the fervent admirer of Balzac, for whom a single reading of the novels is to change the face of the world for ever, the theatres of Paris must still be peopled, if not with his heroes, at least with their kind. From Paris to London is but a step, and in our English capital this old sense of the theatre still obtains, although

55

Buzz, Buzz !

precariously. In London it is still possible to imagine an excitement of the auditorium as distinct from the interest of the scene. You would not swear that the blond, adventurous, tired exquisite on your right will not with a bullet put an end to the *ennui* of this and all other evenings. It is not certain that the admirable doll on your left will not figure in next day's *faits divers*. In the gallery some budding pale assassin leers at his patron in the stalls, beneath him Des Esseintes supports a shaky lorgnon, Valmont eyes a malicious Madame de Merteuil, the Courpières and the Contras abound. Or say Picasso's criticism of the town in his *London Music-Hall*, or a reproduction of Beardsley's *At the Opera*, with every conceivable horror in human flesh brought together for our savouring. An audience to be whipped to appetite by Yvette Guilbert at her rawest, to do honour to the music-hall of Huysmans.

How does it go, this famous description of a singer, so full of the theatre for whosoever loves the theatre, so disconcerting for the Puritan and the country cousin ?

Le chef d'orchestre leva son bâton, les musiciens soufflèrent, une femme fit son entrée, se cassa comme une marionnette, et, debout devant le trou du souffleur, donnant de temps à autre un coup de pied dans sa traîne qui l'embarrassait, partit en mesure. Elle était enveloppée d'une robe rose très décolletée, et ses bras nus et encore rouges étaient blanchis par de la poudre. Son menton projetait une ombre sur le bas de son cou. Elle accompagnait le graillement de son

56

gosier avec quatre gestes : une main sur le cœur et l'autre
collée le long de la jambe,—le bras droit en avant, le gauche
en arrière,—le même mouvement effectué en sens inverse,—
les deux mains enfin se tendant ensemble vers le public.
Elle dégoisait un couplet à gauche de la scène, un autre à
droite.   Ses yeux se fermaient et se rouvraient, suivant que
la musique qu'elle rabotait devait toucher les âmes ou les
égayer.   De loin, de la place où Désirée et Auguste étaient
assis, sa bouche grande ouverte, quand elle hurlait le dernier
vers du refrain, béait comme un trou noir.

Pendant un instant quand la musique joua seule la ritour-
nelle, elle toussotta, montrant un profil qu'on ne soupçonnait
pas lorsqu'elle était de face, guigna de l'œil le ménétrier en
chef, regarda ses gants à huit boutons dont les pointes étaient
roidies par l'empois des sueurs, puis elle se pencha sur
l'orchestre, et, gueulant de toute sa voix, elle se secouait les
bras, et une sorte de fumée noire flottait dans le ravin entrevu
sous son aisselle.

La salle entière délira, des acclamations forcenées couru-
rent, et, s'inclinant, souriant, envoyant des baisers, elle faisait
onduler par le remuement de sa hanche sa robe dont la soie
du bas luisait plus éclatante et comme plus neuve que celle
du corsage moins crûment frappée par les feux de la rampe.

Elle versa sa dernière note.   Les bocks scandèrent sur le
bois des planchettes, la charge sonnée furieusement par un
trombone.   La femme s'inclina derechef, fit voir ses deux
pis réunis dans la digue de son corsage et séparés par une
fente où perlaient des gouttes, et, ramassant sa jupe avec les
poings, elle batifola du museau et, trottinant, s'enfuit, assourdie
par une mitraille de bravos et de bis.

Désirée était pâle d'admiration.   D'abord ces couplets
étaient poignants, il y avait une femme qui pleurait son enfant
mort et maudissait la guerre, et l'on n'entend pas des choses
aussi émouvantes sans que les larmes vous montent aux yeux,
puis la chanteuse lui paraissait belle comme une reine, avec

Buzz, Buzz !

ses bracelets, ses pendeloques et la queue mouvante de sa
jupe ; elle se rendait bien compte que les joues étaient
recrépies et les yeux bordés, mais aux lumières, dans cet
éblouissement du décor, cette femme enchantait quand même
avec son luxe de chairs mastiquées et de soies peintes. Auguste
voguait aussi en plein enthousiasme. Ce rêve impossible à
réaliser pour un homme honnête et pauvre, posséder à soi
pendant un quart d'heure une fille aussi en vue, une fille
aussi éclatante de jeunesse apprêtée et de grâce, lui troubla
la cervelle, et il contemplait la scène vide, les yeux agrandis
et la bouche ouverte. Désirée trouva que cette admiration
devenait inconvenante et elle le pinça. . . .[1]

---

[1] " The conductor raised his stick, the orchestra broke into its opening bars,
and a woman advanced down the stage to the prompter's box, bowing as a
marionette bows, with the apparent intention of breaking herself in half.
Then, giving a backward kick to her train, she began. She was swathed in a
rose-coloured dress of which the bodice was cut low. Her red arms were
smothered in chalk. Her chin threw a shadow on the lower part of her neck.
To match the raucous sounds which issued from her throat she had four
gestures ; one hand on the heart, the other down by her thigh,—right arm in
front, left arm behind,—the same action reversed,—both hands stretched out
towards the public. She bawled the verses left and right alternately, opening
and shutting her eyes according as the rasping melody was doleful or trivial.
From the back rows, where sat Désirée et Auguste, her mouth, wide open
for the last verse, had all the blackness of a cavern.

" She used the intervals between the verses, during which the orchestra
mumbled the symphony, to clear her throat, exhibit a profile which her full-face
would not have led you to suspect, ogle the first violin, and snatch a glance at
her eight-buttoned gloves, of which the fingers were stiff with dried sweat.
Then, leaning forward over the well of the orchestra and bawling at the top of
her voice, she gesticulated in such manner that the spectators caught glimpses
of what you would have said were wreaths of smoke floating in the pit of
each arm.

" The audience applauded with wild fury, and the woman bowing, smiling and
kissing her hands, waggled her hips to show to better advantage the dress of
which the silk skirt, lit up by the footlights, shone with a greater appearance
of freshness than the bodice.

" She gave off her last note. The spectators thumped the tables in front of
them with the bottoms of their glasses ; the trombone triumphantly sounded
the refrain for the last time. The woman bowed once more, this time so low
as to show below the line of her corsage the nipples between which dripped

58

The Pros and Cons

It may be argued that human nature is the same in all countries and in all times—" All the world over " used to be the phrase. To which I would reply that the maker of the proverb did not know his human nature, and that it is a far cry from the *Folies-Bobino* to a People's Palace at, say, Leeds. In the provincial theatre everybody knows his neighbour or divines him, and there is scant sense of peril. Stalls and Circle do a daylight business together. The whistler in the gallery is your butcher-boy, the giggler in the pit your washerwoman. Every member of the audience would appear to be in possession of a passport of respectability visé'd by the police. There is not an emotion in the house that would surprise you ; political tracts in the guise of novels are thumbed in the intervals.

But it is not to be imagined that the provincial finds humiliation in his provincial quality. He

---

beads of sweat. Then picking up her skirt and with a last grin and smirk she trotted off to a deafening cannonade of bravos and ' Encores ! '

" Désirée was pale with admiration. To begin with, the verses had a sense of sentimentality. They were all about a woman robbed of her child and cursing war ; moving things like this are not to be heard without tears coming into your eyes. Again, the singer seemed to her to be lovely as a queen, with all her bracelets and ornaments and the undulating skirt. It was obvious that the cheeks were rouged and the eyelashes pencilled, but what with the lights and the scenery the woman seemed to get some sort of enticement into her made-up fleshiness and painted silks.

" Auguste, too, was completely carried away, troubled by the desire—impossible of realization to a man of his respectability and humble means—the desire to possess if only for a few minutes a singer of such notoriety, a woman of such rejuvenated grace. With wide-open mouth and round, staring eyes he continued to gaze at the empty stage. Désirée held such admiration to be improper, and gave her lover a pinch."

Buzz, Buzz !

glories in it, with or without your leave. I could not if I would deliver a better attack on the provinces than the defence of them contained in Dixon Scott's explanation of Mr. Arnold Bennett:

> The Metropolitan view-point is inevitably as oddly askew as London itself is on the map; the Londoner sees life, England's life, at an angle, fore-shortened, as from a stage-box; instead of taking to it gradually, breast-on, from the primitive beach, every step an adventure, he nips into it aslant, deep water at once, from the door of his sophisticated bathing-van—a solid half of experience irrecoverably missed. And thus, as a consequence, the provinces are always for him a kind of vague hinterland, protoplasmic and grey, an illimitable East End somewhere at the back of the shires; and even if he doesn't actually ask wearily, with Mr. Walkley, " What *are* the Five Towns anyway ? " he does feel that the proper tone to speak of the provinces artistically is a sort of Gissing greyness, as who should talk of Soup Kitchens and the Submerged. A Pottery *Il Penseroso* he can understand, but not a Pottery *L'Allegro*.

I should be content to add only to this that the provincial is a poor wader, with little inclination for an attack on the London beach. In this matter of the theatre he is content to remain buried in his home-provinces, taking very much what comes. And what *does* come ?

Once in a life-time Coquelin, once every decade Sarah Bernhardt, in a music-hall snippet Réjane, and Duse never at all. As who should say the modern painters with Whistler, Sargent, and Augustus John left out. Coming to our native fry, I could mention a score of stage-worthy actors who are

60

never to be seen out of London. Writing at some distance from the newspaper files, one cannot be absolutely sure of one's facts, and therefore it may be that Norman McKinnell and Gerald du Maurier, Henrietta Watson and Nina Boucicault have buried themselves from time to time in what actors term " the country "; but we may take them as types of the competent West End actors who alone make bearable the West End type of play. To the provincial playgoer, the polished acting of such players as these is unknown. He is confirmed in his championship of the Potteries, let us say, and of the acting indigenous thereto by comparison of the native article with the travesties of London actors who tour the provinces wearing the shirt-fronts of their masters with so impudent a differ-ence. It is significant that the fifth-rate London actor in Somebody's " No. 1 Company " is neither better dressed nor better mannered than the butter-merchant whom he would amaze. Incredible though it would appear, I have even seen the fifth-rate London actress in what is called a Smart Society Play or the Success of the London Season more dowdily dressed than her sisters in the three-and-sixpenny Circle.

There is perhaps a providence in this. Who knows but that your provincial, were he to be flooded with the full glory of London acting, might sicken of his provincial makeshifts and so die ? As it is, he leaves the theatre at the municipal striking of eleven o'clock, cheered by the serried

Buzz, Buzz !

ranks of cabs (half a dozen), taxis (three), private carriages and motors (one each), which are the provincial equivalent for the bustle of the London streets at the loosing of the theatres.

The Case For

We cannot, however, dispose of the Provincial Stage by condemning its theatres as meeting-houses of mediocrity, its actors as the perambulatory unfashionable, its plays as the remainder from yester-year. Your provincial, as Mr. Bennett is never tired of telling the rest of the world, is a person of gumption and has a way of his own of dealing with what, to the Londoner, would be a depressing situation. Faced with a theatre in which it was a moot-point as to whether the lifting of the curtain tended to raise the spirits of the spectator or to depress them still further, the provincial made up his mind to make a bid for independence with a theatre of his own. You must realise that there was nothing rash or precipitate about such a decision. It was the result of much quiet cogitation. For some years the provincial has been discovering that the Londoner prefers your smart, safe actor to the nobly adventurous ; that to the greatest Shakespearean actor of our time he will prefer the lavish voicelessness of Sir Herbert Tree ; that to the schoolgirls he will hand over without protest such a past-master of wistfulness

The Pros and Cons

as Mr. Martin Harvey,[1] such a high priest of dignified tushery as Mr. Lewis Waller.[2]

Besides making these quiet discoveries, the provincial had long realised that it was he and not the Londoner who was in the habit of putting his hand into his pocket on behalf of the theatre's forlorn hopes. In the provinces alone had there been on view at any time during the last twenty years a Lear, a Coriolanus, and a Caliban, not in manner majestical and revivalistic, but in the ordinary romantical, catchpenny way of business. In the provinces alone had there been on view— and this is the forlorn part of the business—a Hedda Gabler, a Hilda Solness, and a Nora plying their unostentatious trade, day in and day out, in small theatres, to scanty and bewildered audiences, for a pittance. Here indeed was pluck of an order unknown to your West End. The rich provincial would preen himself as he bought tickets for the nursery governess.

Then came the day when the provincial woke up to realise that he had in all probability to wait another two years for the new Pinero about which all London and the morning papers were talking.

---

[1] A distinguished critic to whom this chapter was submitted in manuscript returned it with a note attacking Mr. Martin Harvey's "wistfulness" in the single phrase "O lor!" Deferentially I submit that in *The Only Way*—the single piece in which I have seen this actor, counting in Elia's phrase the fifth act of *Hamlet* as nothing—the hoarse utterance, the dragging delivery, the exaggerated self-pity, the Irvingesque melancholy are masterly. Provided always that the actor has a diversity of gear in his wardrobe.

[2] Always a much better actor than his admirers would allow us to believe. His Beaucaire was a performance of great finish and beauty.

Buzz, Buzz !

Straightway and magnificently he decided that the time had come for him to run a theatre and, if need be, a Pinero of his own. But, being a provincial and, therefore, as Mr. Bennett would assure us again, a 'cute and canny fellow, he did not go the length of running his theatre in the sensible, straightforward way, *i.e.* out of the rates, but put it about, as they say, that if any high-souled, foolish person was prepared to lose money in the establishment of a Repertory Theatre, he, the provincial, was equally disposed to—look benevolently on. Never was venture more tenderly nursed. The critics made it a point of honour to temper the mildest breezes. Theories they stretched to breaking point and beyond. Dingy parlours with forests of Welsh dressers—a cheap line in point of production— were declared to be the only setting for dramatic action. The King's English—not always obtainable at three pounds a week—was held to verge on the pedantic and to be no longer indispensable as a means of tragic communication. Following upon Mr. Masefield's *Nan*, a spurious Somersetshire dialect became the settled lingo of the Repertory playwright. (That the scene was laid in Warwickshire or Lancashire did not affect the accent by the breadth of a diphthong.) A cheapening management abolished the harmless, necessary theatre-orchestra in favour of alleged intellectual conversation between the acts. A fatherly Town Council, or that part of it which gets itself elected to the Committee for watching over and diminishing

the people's pleasures, decided that critical conversation could not be expected to sustain itself on
beverages stronger than cocoa. The result of all
these prohibitions and limitations was that before
the Repertory Theatre had been going a month,
its auditorium had come closely to resemble one's
idea of a *morgue*, the moribund and comatose
spectators preserved in some semblance of life by
the thin trickle of interest from the stage. Finally,
Sir Herbert Tree sought to laugh the Repertory
Theatres out of existence with his famous riddle,
" When is a Repertory Theatre not a Repertory
Theatre ? " with its devastatingly witty answer,
" When it's a success."

Piqued to exasperation, certain of the Repertory
Theatres decided that at all costs they must turn
their successes of esteem to successes with a good,
solid ring about them. To which end they closed
their programmes to all but the immaturities—
very little troubling or perplexing these—of way-
ward genius, and the feebler productions of the
eminent hack-writers. Their descents were less
popular than their soarings. Not to pursue an
ungrateful subject at too tedious a length, let it
suffice to state that no failure could have been
greater than the attempt of the Repertory Theatres
to compete with the theatre proper. On the lowest
levels the commercial theatre need never fear a
rival. . . . Soon even the pretence to a repertory
disappeared. A Repertory Theatre, I take it, is
a theatre which has a repertory, and I also take it

65

Buzz, Buzz !

that that repertory should be representative of the best pieces of the theatre in all its stages of development. That is to say, that a foreigner who took his English literally would expect to witness during a year of attendance at a Repertory Theatre frequent and regular performances of *Caste, The School for Scandal, The Way of the World, A New Way to pay Old Debts, Macbeth, Hedda Gabler, The Voysey Inheritance, The Gay Lord Quex, Magda, The Importance of being Earnest, Hamlet,* and *Charley's Aunt.*[1] Such a foreigner would be disappointed. He might be able to see one of these plays once, or every night for a week till he was sick of it, but without any likelihood of ever seeing it again. In a word, the Repertory Theatre became a theatre without a repertory, where a stock company of middling players produced for runs of a week at a time plays of a nondescript mediocrity.

And yet, in spite of lessening zest and decreasing interest, it is to be maintained that the whole value of the provincial stage in the last ten or fifteen years has lain in its Repertory Theatres. Much of their later work may have been a mistake, but the whole of the earlier part of it was plucky, well-intentioned, and even magnificent. One would wish for nothing better than, in front of the curtain, the comparatively intelligent and receptive London audience, and, behind the curtain, the plays produced by the

---

[1] I do NOT claim that this is a list of the Best Twelve Plays or anything like it. They are taken more or less haphazard, the intention being to represent *the kind of* repertory a Repertory Theatre should possess.

The Pros and Cons

provincial repertory theatres during the first five years of their existence, or by the Birmingham Repertory Theatre [1] to the end of 1916, when these lines were written. In these circumstances one would at a pinch be willing to accept the repertory standard of acting. And here one would entreat the reader to be ready with his pinch of salt. One would entreat him not to take the author too heavy-handedly. It has been said that criticism should be constructive as well as destructive. (There was once a Political Society entitled *The Constructive Pessimists*, but it is not recorded that the enthusiastic President and optimistic Secretary ever succeeded in adding a third to their number.) In very much the same way constructive criticism of repertory acting must always labour under great difficulties. That incomparable prig in the play, Pryce Ridgeley, was astonished, in view of the stipends of the minor

---

[1] Analysis of the programmes of the Birmingham Repertory Theatre between February 1913 and July 1916 shows frequent performances of—

The Tempest.	W. Shakespeare.
Twelfth Night.	W. Shakespeare.
A New Way to pay Old Debts.	Philip Massinger.
The Clandestine Marriage.	George Colman and David Garrick.
The Liar.	Samuel Foote.
She Stoops to Conquer.	Oliver Goldsmith.
The Critic.	R. B. Sheridan.
The Importance of being Earnest.	Oscar Wilde.
The Liars.	Henry Arthur Jones.
Candida.	George Bernard Shaw.
The Silver Box.	John Galsworthy.
The Pigeon.	John Galsworthy.
The Voysey Inheritance.	Granville Barker.
The Tragedy of Nan.	John Masefield.
David Ballard.	Charles McEvoy.

Analysis of the programmes of Miss Horniman's Company in Manchester

Buzz, Buzz !

clergy, " to get the Gospel preached as satisfactorily as we do." I can never go to a repertory performance without one half of me being amazed at the general level of adequacy among the actors and the other half of me disliking that level exceedingly. In other words, repertory acting is bad absolutely and good relatively. It is good " considering." And the explanation is simple. A Repertory Theatre is known to exist for the production of plays which cannot get a hearing on the commercial stage, *i.e.* which cannot draw a house. In that foreknowledge a house refuses to be drawn, which

---

between September 1907 and December 1915 shows a number of performances of—

Hippolytus.	Euripides.
The Trojan Women.	Euripides.
Measure for Measure.	W. Shakespeare.
The Comedy of Errors.	W. Shakespeare.
Every Man in his Humour.	Ben Jonson.
She Stoops to Conquer.	Oliver Goldsmith.
The School for Scandal.	R. B. Sheridan.
Man and Superman.	George Bernard Shaw.
Major Barbara.	George Bernard Shaw.
The Voysey Inheritance.	Granville Barker.
Prunella.	Laurence Housman and Granville Barker.
The Silver Box.	John Galsworthy.
The Pigeon.	John Galsworthy.
The Cloister.	Émile Verhaeren.
The Tragedy of Nan.	John Masefield.
David Ballard.	Charles McEvoy.
Hindle Wakes.	Stanley Houghton.

These plays, which are the nucleus of a large body of admirable effort, approximate very closely to my imaginary list. The best work of the Manchester Company was done between 1907 and 1912, since which date the programmes have shown a constantly diminishing enterprise and courage. To the Birmingham Company belongs the honour of never having lowered the flag of fine things ; nor have they tolerated the performance of rubbish by visiting companies. A magnificent record.

The Pros and Cons

is what Euclid or Herbert Spencer or Sir John Lubbock meant by declaring action and reaction to be equal and opposite. Hence the employment at modest salaries of " repertory " actors, by which one means a celebrity on the down-grade or a humble person who has never climbed. It is not implied that these actors act any the worse for being paid small money or that the commercial actor acts any better for being paid big money. It should be evident, however, that fashionable players adjudged by public opinion to be good actors and great players who have forced public opinion to follow in their wake are able to command higher salaries than a Repertory Theatre can afford. So the Repertory Theatre has to take what is left. At the same time it must be stated definitely and without any possible shadow of misunderstanding that to the credit of the Repertory Theatre we must put many pieces of acting which have been absolutely as well as relatively fine. No sincere and honest critic of our day can have had a rarer or more exquisite pleasure than that occasioned by their discovery.

Popular Fallacies

THAT ALL FRENCH PLAYS ARE AMUSING

IT was my fortune not so very long ago to spend the better part of two years in the most picturesque, that is to say, the dullest, humanly speaking, part of the south of France—the *villes mortes* dear to the heart of the antiquarian, the dead-and-alive cities of the Gulf of Lions : Arles, Tarascon, Avignon, and Nîmes. It was during the war, and the theatres would open one night in fifty. Stuffy little holes all of them, built on lines of greatest resistance to the comfort of the playgoer. Boxes cut slit-wise at right-angles to the stage, like the galleries of a tennis-court. Circles of which the double row of benches offers choice of discomfort—either the absence of knee-room compels the uniform inclination of spectators half-right or half-left, or the proximity to the roofing enforces a craning of necks not to be explained by the proceedings on the stage.

In the course of something under two years' playgoing I struck — there is no other word for the accidence of these adventures—I struck, then, *Horace* and *Le Malade Imaginaire* ; *La Tosca* with piano accompaniment ; *Manon*, ditto ; *L'Aiglon* without Sarah Bernhardt ; *Le Mariage de Mdlle. Beulemans* with the ever-delightful Dieudonné ; that devastating inanity, *La Petite Chocolatière* ; and, I think, five plays by MM. Flers and Cavaillet, of which I only remember *Primerose*,

Popular Fallacies

Papa, *L'Ane de Buridan*, and *Le Bois Sacré*. These
twelve performances made up the budget of my
playgoing, a *revue*, advertised in disgraceful phrase
as featuring " la célèbre créatrice du Pas de l'Ours
et du Tipperary " and as being of such propriety
that whole families could see it, failing to draw a
quorum. Those of us who had sadly assembled
were given tickets for a performance two months
ahead and bidden to go our ways. If from this
programme you take away the classics and the
pianistic orgies, there remains for discussion—since
no one wants to argue about Rostand at his most
boring but one, the acknowledged little Belgian
masterpiece, or sheer drivel — there remains for
discussion MM. Flers and Cavaillet.

One of the greatest stumbling-blocks to colla-
boration has always seemed to me to be the im-
probability of two persons continuing to think in
agreement for any prolonged period about quite
different things. MM. Flers and Cavaillet have got
over this difficulty by agreeing to continue to think
of the same play under different settings and names.

Primerose, for instance, is a young lady of good
family moving in good circles. At least they have
a bishop or an eminence of sorts to dinner. At
this dinner-party the young lady's fiancé discovers
that he has lost his fortune and that it would be
an improper thing for him, in the circumstances, to
go on being engaged to the young lady. To
gratify an exaggerated sense of disinterestedness,
he proceeds calmly to throw her over. (Actually

Buzz, Buzz !

there is very little calmness about it, that quality being unknown to the French *jeune premier*.) Whereupon the young lady to a nunnery, the bishop or cardinal consenting. The hero returned from America, whither he has exiled himself for just so long as it takes to pick up a fortune in that astonishing country, finds the novice within a hair's-breadth of becoming a nun. Literally within a hair's-breadth, the young person's tresses being due for shearing on the morrow. The *chevelure* and the young person's retention of it to the last possible minute do the trick. She lets her hair down in the presence of her former lover, who declares his undying and never even moribund affection. Whereupon the young lady, throwing her devotions to the winds, leaps into his arms, the bishop or cardinal conniving. Charming philosophy which would make the convent a *pis aller* for the disappointed ! And yet this artless piece of blasphemy filled the Comédie Française to overflowing.

Papa is about a young lady who prefers her fiancé's well-preserved father to the callow youth himself. . . .

L'Ane de Buridan is about a young gentleman who is unable to make up his mind between rival mistresses and gets out of the difficulty by marrying an innocent young thing who climbs into his bedroom window at four o'clock in the morning with a proposal to go fishing.

Each of these plays may be described as artless to the point of cretinism.

Popular Fallacies

In *Le Bois Sacré* the authors present a study of nymphomania which is really rather more for grown-ups. It is depressing, however, to think that the French stage, or the more popular part of it, should have no choice save as between a naïveté bordering on the lunatic and the undisguised erotic.

During my fairly frequent visits to sea-coast towns I made regular visits to the theatres, not so much in hope of seeing good plays as of getting away from the crowds of Arabs, Cochin-Chinese, negroes, half-castes, prostitutes, souteneurs and their kind which litter the ports of Southern Europe. But the theatres brought little relief. One found oneself hedged in by comic opera ; not the breezy, tuneful, honest British sort, but the vapid buffooneries of the relentless overproduction of which French critics have always complained. Three-quarters of a century ago the wittiest of them called these swarms of *operettes*, musical sparrows. " Sparrows hatched without intermission, come hail, rain or snow, welcomed or ignored by the public, in the profusion or dearth of singers, undeterred alike by the siege of Sebastopol or the Plague." Alas that criticism of the biting, semi-libellous sort is no more the vogue ! Alas that it would no longer be considered in the best of taste to put up a notice *Il est défendu de faire de la musique contre ce mur !* Fortunately our native English wit, despite its heavy-handedness, is capable on occasion of doing considerable damage. Take as example that famous English critic who, abandoning a clamorous and

73

over - strident Juliet to fourth - act hysterics, was
discovered attempting to bribe a policeman on
point-duty to be allowed to take his place.

" Let me," he was overheard to say, " relieve
you of a tedious job. There is a noise in mine
ears which I would drown with the rumble of these
so pleasant carts ! "

Creak they never so loudly, move they never so
woodenly, these British carts and lorries cannot
lumber and jolt in more distressing fashion than
the drama with which I made acquaintance in the
south of France.

That all French Acting is competent

It is probable that many a sturdy Briton owes
his first experience of French acting to one of the
occasional but always ravishing descents upon our
shores of Madame Sarah Bernhardt. It is equally
probable that his first glimpse of French plays
should have been afforded by the world-weary
and surely travel-weary Lady of the Camellias.
Presuming the sturdy Briton to have had any
coherence, sanity, or power of apprehension left to
him after the devastating passage through his senses
of the great French genius, they, the remnant of
his critical faculties, will of a surety have found a
rallying-point in the antics of the wretch supplying
the Armand. To this perturbed and hysterical
French lover your Briton may be imagined as
clinging grimly ; holding on as to a slippery witness

to be produced in the case shaping in his mind for respectable British acting as against the neurotic and over-excitable French. It is understood, in a shamefaced sort of way, that the want of reserve, the " rant," the " un-Englishness " of the great actress may be pardoned. For people who like that sort of thing, as one of Sir Arthur Pinero's beldams remarks, there is the Continent ! And the Continent has pronounced *nemine contradicente* in its favour.[1] But this cross-Channel mannikin with his jerks and starts, this deranged amorist and hysterical *exalté*, this Chevalier des Grieux in kid gloves and a silk hat—no, your sturdy Briton is not going to put up with so much of a good thing as all that comes to.

Your Briton has but to air his homely wits abroad for a time and he will, if he be a perceiving fellow, realise that there is much in the deportment and gesture of these despised Armands which is true to race and is not merely over-measure. And no sooner will he have made up his mind to concede a certain excess of gesticulation and emphasis—say a hundred per cent above his home standard—than he will begin to perceive that the concession is needed not by the best French actors but by the worst. French male tragic acting has always seemed to me to be their worst—an affair of bellowing and butchery, demanding the utmost of our

[1] We in England have had our dissentients. Was there not once a patroness of the intellectual drama who declared superbly, with reference to Madame Bernhardt, that she did not care for " that kind of acting " ?

allowance. Where no concession is needed is with your French comedian, who can be as nobly undemonstrative as the most insular. " You could see the first dawn of an idea stealing slowly over his countenance, climbing up by little and little, with a painful process, till it cleared up at last to the fulness of a twilight conception—its highest meridian. He seemed to keep back his intellect, as some have had the power to retard their pulsation. The balloon takes less time in filling than it took to cover the expansion of his broad moony face over all its quarters with expression." This is Lamb on Dodd, but it might equally serve for Coquelin as the befogged interpreter in *L'Anglais tel qu'on le parle*. " A glimmer of understanding would appear in the corner of his eye, and for lack of fuel go out again. A part of his forehead would catch a little intelligence, and be a long time in communicating it to the remainder." Would not this do for Coquelin's M. Jourdain, or Perrichon, or the tender-hearted old fribble in *Frou-frou*, or any other of the tribe of worldly simpletons ?

> Let me see if Philip can
> Be a little gentleman

runs the old rhyme in " Shock-headed Peter," and it is true that the best French actors can behave with the *retenue* of French gentlemen, very nearly with the phlegm of our English sort. It is the indifferent *jeune premier*, trying to wrest every ounce of insipidity out of a wretched part, who is the trouble. These young men always remind me of Du Maurier's drawing in *Punch* depicting a sitting-out couple in sentimental pose. The swain would appear to be delivering himself of a deathless phrase. " You would hardly believe it," he is really saying, " but from this house to the Marble Arch is exactly one mile." The phlegmatic Briton who had no French would find it hard to believe that the passionate young gentleman, divesting himself of his overcoat, was not a prey to all those tribulations which plucked the harness from Antony.

> O ! cleave, my sides !
> Heart, once be stronger than thy continent.
> Crack thy frail case ! . . . bruised pieces, go ;
> You have been nobly borne,

the fellow would appear to be saying, as he hands the coat to his man. Then will he change to an excess of sprightliness, a fidgety compound of Malvolio and Puck. He will scan his phrases foot by foot, with hand and arm extended, a pinch of atmosphere held firmly between forefinger and thumb. He will *conduct* a speech with the beat of a *chef d'orchestre*. He will shoot his linen with the prestige of a conjuror. He will pace a drawing-room like a tiger his cage. And this in Act I., at the very beginning of the imbroglio. For him no possibility of a *crescendo*. . . . Your French *ingénue* is better. There is a composure about the archness of these sophisticated minxes. " What colour are the eyes of your mistress ? " is the remark of a chit from school to the young *dépravé* she is about

77

Buzz, Buzz!

to marry, the composed delivery of which would stagger a British audience. " We English," says Mr. Max Beerbohm somewhere, " are not in the habit of alluding to our *ingénues*. It would be brutal." Perhaps the less said about the French *jeune premier*, the more tactful. For we must remember that the French are our allies.

The Two Voices

A Conversation

Scene.—The Winter Garden of the Hotel Superb
in a manufacturing town in the north of England.
One of the disputants, aged fifty-six, is a Playwright of the Intellectual School, to the credit of
whose minor plays may be put actual stage-runs
of as much as a fortnight. In his desk, unacted,
is the most sinister comedy since *John Gabriel
Borkman*. If this personage has an intellectual
fault, it is an exaggerated reverence for self-control,
or, to put it another way, it is probable that he
would violently disapprove of the writings of Abel
Hermant. He has a feeling for style as delicate as
Henry James and the subtlest sense of the value
of the written word. He has never known a tawdry
or ignoble emotion, and is therefore supremely
unfitted to write plays for the English stage. In
the perfect modesty of his own opinion he is
a commonplace Englishman, representative of his
time, and essentially qualified to produce plays
for the delectation of his peers. He has as great
a dislike to being dubbed intellectual as Charles
Lamb had to being called gentle. The key to him
is his firm conviction that his plays are the shortest
possible cut to the pulsing heart of the public.
The other disputant is a professional critic, the
Playwright's junior by twenty years. Little is
known of this speaker, but as his opinions alone
are in question, more material knowledge is not

79

Buzz, Buzz !

required. It is surmised that whatever his means, his cigars are beyond them. He keeps himself going with stiffish doses of brandy and water. Having fewer ideas, he is the bigger talker.

The discussion is conducted amid the buzz of waiters, the cackle of afternoon tea-takers, recalling Huysmans' phrase, " la sottise innée des femmes," and the, one would think, totally unnecessary adjurations of a loud-voiced female, " Sink, red sun ! " Basket chairs, tea-tables, frippery.

Time.—An afternoon in July 1914.

The usual preliminaries to conversation, offers of tea, cigarettes, etc., and then :

Critic. It's good to see you, my dear fellow. Ten minutes' talk ought to clear up a good many points between us.

Playwright. I hope so. Tell me, what did you mean by " The Repertory Theatre is still-born " ?

Critic. I should have written, " The play of ideas is still-born." The function of the theatre is to create emotion and present it in unequivocal form. The drama of ideas is too much taken up with the " questionable shape," the production of monsters after the order of Gregers Werle, Torvald Helmer, and the Rev. James Mavor Morell.

Playwright. Surely the whole point of these fellows is their normality ? They are naturalness itself. They grow before your eyes. I suppose you are not going to deny that growth is one of the main functions of the dramatist ?

The Two Voices

Critic. By no means. Only I insist that growth and the spectator's apprehension of growth must be a joint affair. Ibsen's habit of last-act revelations of material events happening before the play begins seems to me to be theatrically mischievous. In other words, whilst the spectator should be alive to the growth of character, he should not have to correct misapprehensions nor revise estimates. He should be able to readjust his values by simple addition.

Playwright. I cannot agree with you. A character may be contradictory or even imperfectly apprehensive of itself. It may be necessary to subtract and divide before proceeding to your additions. Why demand a clearer vision in the spectator than in the creator of the character?

Critic. Because cloudy apprehension and imperfect grasp on the part of an author necessarily invest his characters with questionable form and so forbid the proper shaping of our emotions.

Playwright. You are arguing in a circle.

Critic. Many excellent arguments have been so conducted. Let us, however, go back to the imperfect grasp of character and the effect of that imperfection on emotion, by which we mean laughter and tears.

Playwright. Yes, let us go back to that. But first, I am not sure whether I can agree that all theatrical emotion must necessarily consist of unclouded laughter or unquenchable tears.

Critic. I do not ask you to agree to anything

so foolish. You may mix laughter with tears or tears with laughter. You may indulge in both at the same moment, because both are the result of perfectly grasped things happening together which also happen to be incongruous. But you cannot laugh and think or cry and think, because thinking means the effort to cope with something imperfectly grasped, and when the mind is in doubt it will have nothing to say to either laughter or tears. Take for a very simple instance the dramatised version of Dostoievski's *Crime and Punishment*. In the play, the youth is made to murder an old woman for the sake of the money by which he hopes to prevent his sister from making a shameful marriage. Here we have a clear case for theatrical emotion, and you are at liberty to weep bucketsful. But in the novel the emotion has a twofold basis, the motive for the murder being partly generous—to the point of insanity, if you will—and partly sordid. And if you remember, Dostoievski gives the baser motive precedence in point of inspiration. Complication becomes excessive and entirely untheatrical, that is to say, preventive of unembarrassed emotion, when the murderer sacrifices the proceeds of his crime to the needs of a drunken ruffian run over in the street. By what effort can the playgoer size up so much complexity at a first hearing ?

Playwright. I suggest that it is worth any play-goer's while to waste a first hearing to be sure of so tremendous a second.

The Two Voices

Critic. Some old fogey, Ruskin, I think, said that if a book was worth reading once, it was worth reading twice. I maintain that if a play is worth seeing twice it should be a pleasurable and sizeable thing to see it once. Of course I admit that the Russian novel is better than any possible melodramatic version of it by just so much as truth is better than mis-statement. The theatre, however, is not a court of justice. If it is a court at all, it is one for the hearing of evidence only. There must not be, I would even say there cannot be, summing up, verdict, or sentence. From which it follows that the more complicated the play, the more highly-prized judged by intellectual standards, the more difficult the theatrical emotion. In other words, you must bring the audience an intellectual step nearer. Which brings me to my point.

Playwright. Come, that's encouraging !

Critic. My point is that whereas the critic is entitled to judge an artistic achievement by the standard of his best intelligence, the playwright is not entitled to assume that intelligence in an audience gathered together at random. I am entitled to say to you, " Your play is dramatic, given a high standard of intelligence in the audience " ; you are not entitled to say, " My play is dramatic," *tout court,* and without any qualification. If you will insist upon intellectual plays you must equally insist upon an audience trained to think. If you are a Shakespeare or writer of universal plays— this class of author is not as small as you would

Buzz, Buzz!

imagine if you go back far enough to include the Greeks—any audience how ordinary soever will do. Now curiously enough to you, naturally enough to me, all the greatest, most dramatic, and most poignant scenes in the history of the drama lie within the comprehension of the simplest boor or bumpkin. I jotted down a few of them the other day whilst waiting for a train. Here's the list (*takes paper from pocket and reads*).

(*a*) The entry of Lear with Cordelia in his arms.

Playwright. I've never seen this done on the stage. I should be surprised if it had any effect with the crowd. You mean it made a great effect on you in reading.

Critic (*severely*). No, I saw it with Benson.

(*Reading.*) (*b*) The "*By Heaven, she's warm*" from *The Winter's Tale*.

Playwright. A self-evident proposition which doesn't move me greatly, I'm afraid. But this is impious.

Critic. It is. Don't interrupt (*resumes reading*).

(*c*) The "*Qu'il mourût!*" of old Horace.

Playwright. Connu, mon cher!

Critic. (*d*) Polly Eccles' broken attempts to tell Esther that her soldier husband is returned safe and sound and the whole of the French play on the same theme—*La Joie fait Peur.*

Playwright. Yes, I remember crying at that like a good 'un, but I foolishly put it down to the acting.

Critic. (*e*) Marguerite Gauthier's dying embrace of her lover.

84

The Two Voices

(*f*) The pretence of the old servant in *The Silver King* that he is neither cold nor hungry, and the foiling of the Spider down by the wharf.

(*g*) The shivering and quaking of *I heard the owl scream and the cricket cry*, and *not* that great wonder and marvel, *out of the theatre*, the later agony of *Macbeth*.

(*h*) The actual killing of Caesar. No audience has ever been known to care about what happens to Brutus and Cassius afterwards.

(*j*) The death of Dubedad and *not* Mr. Shaw's perorating.

(*k*) Olivia's farewell to her little sister and brother before she runs away, and the Vicar's finding of her.

(*l*) Any of Henry Irving's farewells or dyings or recognitions of long-lost sons or assumptions of another's guilt.

(*m*) The last line of Wilde's *A Woman of no Importance*, and, of course, the famous

(*n*) *Lady Teazle, by all that's damnable!*

The average audience, as Lamb long ago pointed out, is entirely indifferent to the marital relations of Sir Peter and his lady, except in so far as the differences between them prove amusing. Both you and Henry James would have made an elaborate psychological affair of it. Whereas the curiosity of your theatrical audience is confined to the simple question, " How will Joseph get out of it ? " What do you say to that ?

Playwright. I say that if it had happened to

85

Buzz, Buzz !

the intellectual playwright, as you call us, to write the Screen Scene, he would have furnished Joseph with his way out and have even hit upon Sir Peter's inevitable line.

Critic. Oh no, you wouldn't, you would have had something abstruse on the theme of " She must have a case. Joseph must have a case. All this has got to be looked into."

Playwright. Of course we don't write for duffers. I suggest that those people who make you grasp everything become bores.

Critic. That's just the point. You've got to write for duffers. You've got to write down to the lowest common feeling of the crowd. Take two Hamlets which we both of us know. Robertson's drew tears, but it wasn't a patch intellectually on Laurence Irving's, which nevertheless depended for its proper appreciation on the spectator being up to all kinds of bizarre and decadent antecedents and correlations. Robertson was exquisite and emotional, but he side-tracked all the knotty bits. Irving — and I suppose we weren't misled — grappled with them all and set us thinking furiously.

Playwright. I remember you wanted to fight me after the " Get thee to a nunnery " scene.

Critic. Exactly. And for the very reason that we couldn't feel in unison about any single line of it, it was less good a theatrical performance than Robertson's, though I should probably agree as to its being the greater intellectual achievement. It was a Hamlet for the study. Now it's your turn !

86

The Two Voices

Playwright. My dear fellow, you go so fast there's no keeping pace with you. To go back a little. What you say about laughter and tears being the result of perfect apprehension is true enough to be illuminating, but surely those people who make you grasp everything become bores ? You must be explicit now and again, of course. I agree that it is well to give your audience an occasional breather, to give them time to look around and take stock. But set their minds to work again as soon as may be ! The emotions are soon blunted, but the brain is insatiable. On the question of standardised intelligence in an audience, I think you are fairly in the centre ; but is it practicable, is it feasible to select even a middle layer and to suggest that the dramatic quality of a play is to stand or fall by the verdict of that layer ? I suggest that in the South Sea Islands, where the natives eat their grandfathers, even *The Silver King* might be considered undramatic.

Critic. You were always a joker. I hold that in temperate zones *The Silver King* is the type of play best suited to a general audience. Shakespeare is only popular in the theatre because he deals in the same themes as *The Silver King*. And if it pleased him to treat the themes nobly instead of tawdrily, he did it in such a way as not to disconcert his audience. There are quite enough of the big simplicities in any play of Shakespeare to float an audience over the evening. There never was a great and popular play that had an intellectual

87

rather than an emotional basis. Galsworthy is ten times the draw Shaw is because there is not an intellectual idea in him from first to last.

Playwright. Shaw is ten times as big a draw as Galsworthy.

Critic. My dear fellow, I must decline to argue with you about statistics. As I was saying, Galsworthy is a very clever writer of plays which are as chock-full of melodrama as the worst excesses of Wilson Barrett. A navvy or a tram-guard would get hold of all the essential in Galsworthy ; whereas he wouldn't have the ghost of a notion with you clever fellows where to begin.

Playwright. Confound you ! I am *not* a clever literary playwright. My plays cannot and do not fail on the stage. It is nice of you to make out my emotions to be rare and noble and yours a mere wallow. I have no doubt that when you go to *The Silver King* after a good dinner you are capable of wallowing. But it's a lapse, or else it's a pure pose. Do you want to suppress altogether what you call the " intellectual " theatre, to which, by the way, I'll deny with my dying breath that I belong ? Plays that are worth acting are worth talking about, and I challenge you to talk to me for ten minutes about *The Silver King*. You couldn't do it ! Whereas I could talk to you for an hour about *Hedda Gabler*.

Critic. Will you swear on your honour that you know what *Hedda Gable* is all about ?

Playwright. I don't know that that really matters.

The Two Voices

I have a ghost of an idea, and a ghost may be a highly attractive thing.

Critic. Not on the stage.

Playwright. And when to the ghost is fitted, superimposed—I want a word that doesn't imply a perfect fit—a plastic, subtle creature, I think you get a bit more of an idea on the stage than you do from the book. There are some tremendously dramatic things in this play, and I am sure that in comparison with Hedda, you would find the Spider's mistress a dull woman. I am not sure that I know a greater play outside Shakespeare. I admit it isn't jolly.

Critic. I am afraid my playgoing brain doesn't work quickly enough for Ibsen. Of course in two or three hundred years when we have all attained a higher degree of theatrical quick-wittedness Ibsen will turn out to have been the greatest dramatist that ever lived. He *is* the greatest dramatist that ever lived—in the study. I will take my coat off and fight you here and now for *John Gabriel Borkman* as the finest play that was ever written—for the study. It's Lamb's case of Lear on the stage as an " old man in a passion." When we read we can *hear* Borkman pacing up and down, year after year, in that tragic room of his upstairs. The house shakes with him. Then think of any Borkman you ever saw on the stage. A broken bankrupt without the pluck to look the world in the face. Whereas he's an eagle with a broken wing !

Playwright. Now that's what I call handsome !

Buzz, Buzz !

(*A pause.*) I think you must let me make my point that until your three hundred years are up, the proper way to write plays is to do as Shakespeare did and start with something that the average man won't jib at. You are then at liberty to enrich it for yourself and your friends. Shakespeare's plots have never given me much pleasure. It's the diction, and I've always thought the Germans must be a dull lot to play him in translations.

Critic. Yes, my friend, and on the stage it's the more grossly effective bits of diction that count. On the stage " Farewell the tranquil mind " is eclipsed by the noise of " Villain, be sure thou prove my love a whore." No actor can give you the infinite regret of

> I am not valiant neither,
> But every puny whipster gets my sword.

Even " Wash me in steep-down gulfs of liquid fire ! " hardly matters. In fact the *words* don't matter. You want the noise of Othello's pain, the physical bellow of a wounded bull. It is said that with Salvini the words were never heard.

Playwright. A good point, but plays are made up of words, and it is words that lead up to the bellow. If Shakespeare hadn't made a beautiful creature of Othello this bellowing would lose a lot of its quality, wouldn't it ? It seems to me as though you were anxious to prove the theatre a common place for common minds.

Critic. And so I think it is. At least I am sure that melodrama is the most satisfactory form of

90

art. You don't give melodrama its proper due. Frédérick-Lemâitre preferred it, and so from all accounts did Kean and Garrick. Then there's Irving's record. They say Flaubert never went to a melodrama without bursting into tears.

Playwright. I remember Mr. Gladstone writing a testimonial for *The Sign of the Cross*, but I do wish you'd point out the passages in *The Grip of Iron* or *The Face at the Window* at which you think Flaubert would have burst into tears.

Critic. Please be serious.

Playwright. I am serious.

Critic. You will not deny, I suppose, that the drama of the great poets is merely melodrama rearranged, that the sublimities of Shakespeare, Racine, Corneille, and Goethe are like the sublimities of Paul or the profundities of Ecclesiastes—sublimities and profundities that a child could fathom ?

Playwright. Certainly in the theatre you return again and again to the profound simplicities, but their greatest effect is attained when you realise that the people who give them utterance are human, and therefore subtle, and not mere sawdust like your Silver Kings. And you must interest as well as move and stun. Pure emotion is so exhausting that without interest you would be done up in a single act.

Critic. I'm not sure about that. My theatrical passions have always been made of the finest part of pure emotion. Let me run over the performances that have made the most impression on me since I

Buzz, Buzz !

was first taken to the theatre at the age of nine. We'll soon see what share intellect has had in the plays I've liked best.

Playwright. Begin then.

Critic. The first performance of which I have a distinct recollection was that of Courtenay Thorpe as Prince Hal and Laurence Irving as Justice Shallow.

Playwright. I didn't see these particular performances, but they are certainly two of the best actors of our time.

Critic. Janet Achurch in *Antony and Cleopatra*.

Playwright. She didn't do it well, but she was certainly an actress of genius. It was the greatness of the play that got at you.

Critic. Wilson Barrett in *The Sign of the Cross*.

Playwright. Tosh ! Rubbish ! Nonsense ! No excuse for you ! Sanity can't defend it.

Critic. I'm giving you autobiography, not criticism. I don't know that I should care to defend the play at my present stage of experience.

Playwright. Go on.

Critic. Henry Irving as Lesurques in *The Lyons Mail*.

Playwright. Lesurques, *not* Dubosc, was one of the old man's finest parts. It used to move me greatly.

Critic. Bernhardt in . . .

Playwright (interrupting). I'll agree to anything you like within reason, or beyond, if it comes to that.

The Two Voices

Critic. Mrs. Patrick Campbell in *Mariana.*

Playwright. Greatly impressed by her Magda, and immensely interested, even excited by her Hedda.

Critic. Hawtrey in *Lord and Lady Algy.*

Playwright. Didn't see.

Critic. Well then, Réjane, Coquelin.

Playwright. You forget I'm a provincial and therefore bound to lack many moving experiences.

Critic. John Hare in *The Gay Lord Quex.*

Playwright. Oh, there I'm tremendously with you.

Critic. Let me see . . . Ellen Terry in *Much Ado About Nothing.*

Playwright. I saw her in almost everything else, but I'm sound.

Critic. Now for the great test. Benson, in a score of plays.

Playwright. I've always said, and you've always said—we two against the world—that he's a great and inspiring actor. . . . Now *is* there very much between us ? You have invited me to consider the " unintellectual " performances which moved you as a boy, and I find and admit that they moved me equally, or almost all of them did. I can't help thinking, as I said before, that your espousal of the " popular " play is something of a pose. You are not the hearty common-place fellow you would like the world to take you for. You are in point of fact highly critical, but you like to give your emotions rather more than their fair share of air and exercise.

93

Buzz, Buzz !

So you shape whatever is before you into emotional guise. It won't suit you to admit it of course, but for the purposes of argument you become an exaggerated you, and would starve me into something more austere than I am. And yet it's you who are the Puritan ! . . . I implore you to abandon this Root-and-Brand attitude. Don't lay down too hard-and-fast rules. Don't deny interest its place in the theatre. Don't banish the rare, the precious, the exquisite. Think how often we have sat together in the theatre, you and I, and held our breaths at some wonderful bit of art, playwright's or actor's, some disregarded miracle brought off in careless indifference to the want of appreciation, for the miracle's own sake. The summer flower is to the summer sweet, you know. Don't banish flowers from our theatre and leave us only the common grass. We are not a nation of farmers. . . . Of course I realise that the dramatist must keep hitting the nail on the head, only let there be beautifully fashioned nails, and let the sledge-hammer be occasional. I cannot agree with you that the dramatist must do nothing else.

Critic (*unrepentant*). Whatever else he does must be accounted a miss. At least the playwright has got to take the risk.

Playwright. We've all got to take risks. (*With persuasion.*) All the same I think there is not a very great deal of difference between us ?

Critic (*grudgingly*). Not as much as I had hoped.

94

The Two Voices

Playwright. It is getting late. Will you dine with me?

Critic. With pleasure. (*Apprehensively.*) You are not contemplating dragging me to *Submergers and Submerged* afterwards?

Playwright. Well, they do say George Robey's at one of the halls.

Critic (*brightly*). Come along, then!

II
Then came each Actor—

Stanley Houghton[1]

I WELL remember the last two occasions on which I saw Stanley Houghton. The first was some months after he had taken the plunge and had come to town in the old story-book way. I was making that, to the provincial, greatest of journeys—though you will never get him to admit it—the run from Euston to one of the Northumberland Avenue hotels, and in St. Martin's Lane came across Houghton. He was in moderately high spirits, and under the shock of unexpected meeting, radiated all that incongruous bundle of naïve immaturities and graceful rawnesses which were the man at that period of his development. He wore jauntily, and with a set, defiant rakishness, the soft sombrero of the poet ; the rest of his attire was palpably that of the provincial man of business. His manner was compounded of a native, abnormal shyness and the sparrow-like assurance of the provincial who in the last ten minutes has conquered the metropolis. He spoke of his immediate work as if it had been hung up by London, and as though he disliked the great city for it. He had not, I thought, much awe and reverence for the capital ; he seemed to resent it as the denizens of the manufacturing towns of the north of England resent Manchester.

He has no feeling that he is provincial, or that the provinces are not the principal asset of England. London he

---

[1] I am aware that Houghton was a playwright and not an actor. But as no book which deals in any way with Repertory Theatres can afford to ignore the writer of their most successful play, and as I can find no other convenient place, the reader is begged to grant room for this playwright among the actors he loved so well.

Buzz, Buzz !

looks upon as a place where rich Lancashire men go for a spree, if they have not time to go to Monte Carlo or Paris. Manchester he looks upon as the centre or headquarters for Lancashire manufacturers, and therefore more important than London. But after all he thinks that Manchester is merely the office for Hindle and the other Lancashire towns, which are the actual source of wealth. Therefore Hindle, Blackburn, Bolton, Oldham and the rest are far more important in his eyes than London or Manchester, and perhaps he is right. Anyhow, the feeling gives him sufficient assurance to stroll into the most fashionable hotels and restaurants, conscious that he can afford to pay for whatever he fancies, that he can behave himself, that he can treat the waiters with the confidence of an aristocrat born—and yet be patently a Lancashire man. He would never dream of trying to conceal the fact, nor indeed could he understand why anybody should wish to try and conceal such a thing.

Thus Houghton in the Introduction to Act I. Scene 3 of *Hindle Wakes*. Certainly our author would never have denied the provinces, and there is no getting away from the damning *and perhaps he is right* in the passage quoted. London was no stimulus to Houghton ; he had exchanged a world he knew intimately for one he knew not at all, and he was gravelled, it seemed to me, for lack of matter. His proper material, we know from the plays, was not the whole of human nature, but that innocently hypocritical, quaintly uncompromising variety we use in the stern manufacturing North. The insolence of life in London, its luxury and ease, its squalor and romance, the everyday imminence of unheard-of happenings made little appeal to Houghton. There was scant material for suburban art

Stanley Houghton

in that perpetual realisation of the incredible which makes any one of the world's capitals a city of the Arabian Nights. And yet Houghton, after the ingenuous manner of Frédéric in Flaubert's *L'Education Sentimentale*, liked to be taken for a man of the world.

The last occasion on which I saw him was at the Hôtel Métropole. He had been to lunch with Mr. Max Beerbohm, *i.e.* to sit for his caricature, and had listened to his host's apologies in anticipation. I can see him now leaning against the mantelpiece, drinking the beer for which his Younger Generation would go to such heroic lengths, and talking with the diffidence and ease, shyness and charm which Mr. Beerbohm was to translate ever so maliciously into a kind of triumphant foolishness.

I am not sure that all the absolutely first-class work done by Houghton is not contained in *Hindle Wakes*, the little sketches *Hawthorn Lodge*, *Grey*, and half-a-dozen others. The rest is mediocre, although redeemed in places by a savage irony worthy of the creator of *Bouvard et Pécuchet*. Take, for instance, the Mrs. Hannah Kennion who objects to the appointment of a Mr. Roberts to the superintendency of the Sunday School on the ground that he is only a working carpenter. Her impossible son says quietly, " It was a carpenter who was crucified, mother." Mrs. Kennion, entirely impervious to the social offence, says superbly, " Please don't be irreverent, Thomas." A remark worthy to rank with Mrs. Jeffcote's " And at Llandudno,

Buzz, Buzz !

too, of all places "—the discussion is of her son's seduction by Fanny—" why, I've been there many a time." Flaubert's *bourgeois* have not bettered these.

Much of his other playwriting is Shaw, Maupassant, and Wilde—the sedulous aping which is the privilege of every budding genius—but it is Shaw with a minimum of wrath and fixity of purpose, Maupassant without the bite, and Wilde without the elegance and social ease. One is inclined to think that this imitativeness was only a feeler after individual expression, since the trick of expressing and not the thing expressed was all the theatre to this playwright of amusement. It is difficult to find any weight of ideas or momentum of sincerity in the plays. The success of *Hindle Wakes* was a gorgeous piece of luck ; its theme was scarcely honest. With a quaint owlishness the guardians of the youth of this country blinkingly maintained that the play did but set forth the immorality of the factory-hand, and, the same laws applying to man as to woman, the blackguard quality of the young mill-owner. What the play actually drew crowds for was the exposition of natural wantonness in a young man, with, in these feminist times, the corollary and plea for equal latitude in the woman. The piece was an enormous *succès de scandale*, and Miss Horniman's theatre was crowded to suffocation. But for the queasy subject there would have been no acclaim. The all but masterly handling, the wonderful insight into Lancashire character, would

Stanley Houghton

not, by themselves and without the sexual appeal, have drawn a house of two. (Those who would deny this do not know the intellectual standards of the provinces.) The rest of the plays are dull and unamusing. They credit their author with little knowledge of the passion, appeasement, and satiety which is all existence ; they show intimacy with the commonplace and the drab, without any inkling of the colour and the crowd of life. And London showed a prime intellectual folly in its acceptance of these other plays ; proof once more that anything with the hall-mark—I had nearly written stigma—of Manchester upon it can impose upon the Metropolis.

It must be said that the plays give little clue to the personality of the man, to that diffidence and charm, that obvious preoccupation with the best-intentioned in life and art, which conquered all those of his critics who knew him intimately, and secured for him so many staunch adherents. Perhaps it is only faint praise of an artist to say that the man was more likeable than his work. But it was certainly that likeableness which disarmed his colleagues of the great Northern daily. They were betrayed, one must think, by sympathy into a too generous leniency. The most obvious criticism of *Fancy Free*, in which the young people talk like assistants at a provincial Selfridge's, must be on the score of manners rather than morals, and yet we find one of our great critics getting into a fume about " canine promiscuity," whereas the

Buzz, Buzz !

play is in scope neither more immoral nor moral than the Congreve or Wilde whom Houghton was trying to imitate. Others of his critics have found in the work of the artist all they admired in the man, and their agreement with his well-known dislike of insipid love-interests blinds them to the fact that he had neither eye nor ear for the banality, the literary commonness, of such a phrase as " About a third of the way through the book *we caught the flicker of a petticoat.*" This kind of false note was never, one must think, very far away from even the best of Houghton's work. . . .

A great deal of stress has been laid, and rightly, on the little story called *Grey*. It reveals a wistfulness, a delicacy of emotion that was rare in the artist and familiar in the man. Houghton was not content with the world he knew ; he laughed at its manners, its morals, its traditions—and he was at home in no other. In Manchester his art had foundation and support ; in the bigger world his work became unsure, and he had hardly found himself again as an artist before he died. It is significant that Houghton went to Paris to escape London and to dream of Manchester ; my chiefest recollection of him is that his spirit was too timid and too retiring to take kindly to a *furore*. He failed as a showman to ride the wave of an advertised success ; he was one of Nature's typical and shyest gentlemen.

Sarah Bernhardt

SARAH BERNHARDT is the last of a line of players whose art is a great and glorious means to no end beyond its own expression and achievement. You may liken such an art to the splashing of unrelated colour, to the roll of verse in an unknown tongue, the naked blare of trumpets. And since the playhouse has a story to tell and we may not be satisfied with abstract sound, however exquisite, with barren fertility of pose and gesture, needs must that we tame the trumpets to a tune, mould sound and colour to the aspect of familiar things. What the story may be would appear not to matter very greatly; and though it were better to see Bernhardt in Racine than in Sardou, it were also better to see her in the worst of her Toscas and Fédoras than any other living actress in no matter what masterpiece of the classic stage.[1]

One comes away from the theatre with the conviction that Marguerite, Adrienne, Frou-Frou, and even Phèdre, when played by a very great actress, must necessarily be one and the same person, and one formulates an easy theory that this is as it should be. Sarah Bernhardt at least takes care that the same violence that is done to the playwright shall

[1] With the possible exception of Ellen Terry in Shakespearean comedy and Eleonora Duse in anything she likes. And yet the art of the latter, for all its exquisite nobility, seems a calculable thing, possible of attainment. Whereas the art of Bernhardt is literally not a calculable thing. Sometimes one thinks that the mind does not enter into it at all, that the actress rises to Phèdre by sheer force of instinct. The penalty of this temperamental fury is that the artist is unfitted—royally if you like—for chillier considerations. I am inclined to think Duse's Adrienne Lecouvreur—which is out of her range—a finer shot at the incompatible than any conceivable effort of Bernhardt's Ibsenwards.

105

be done to humanity. That she will tear a passion to tatters for the glorification of her unexampled virtuosity is an old charge ; it is not so often urged that out of equal malice she will pitch whole scenes in so low a key as to extinguish whatever dramatic interest they may possess. She will fuse whole scenes into an opalescent, ineffable haze. You would know a scene of Bernhardt's if you met it in your dreams. . . .

Recent years' playing of *La Dame aux Camélias* has given rise to a trifle of apprehension for the security of the player's fame. Fulness of tone has gone out of the acting, and only the harmonics remain. One is a little jealous lest their very exquisiteness may make for ineffectiveness in an audience of whom many must for the first time be putting to the touch an inherited wonder of the Bernhardt legend. One has been a little doubtful of the complete triumph in the circumstances of passion etherealised and whittled away to the last wistfulness. In one line alone has the actress never failed to fulfil prophecy, the " Armand ! ce n'est pas toi ; il est impossible que Dieu soit si bon ! " a line always delivered by her in conscious animality of rapture and with a calculated sense of the hunger of the great cats. Here as of old is the glimpse of Blake's " fearful symmetry," and we are conscious once more of the old trepidation at ruthlessness of passion from which spirituality, mentality even, have been wiped away. Without this cry the audiences of to-day had seen only half that art which has put a girdle round the world, that half which is all purged innocence and inviolate ecstasy.

Of this actress's Phèdre the late W. T. Arnold wrote : " It is melancholy to think that a hundred years hence no one will know how Mme. Bernhardt used to say these verses." Nearly half a century has passed since these lines were written, and the actress is using Racine's masterpiece to stir and kindle yet another generation. It is matter for wonder, come to think of it, that this noble and fiery spirit twin with Rachel's should have been housed in so indomitable a frame, should have been dowered with so heroic a quality of persistence. " Garrulous to the very last," wrote Whitman proudly, and there is another verse of the American poet in which we may find an image for the late performances of this great player :

That should I after death invisibly return,
Or long, long hence in other spheres,
There to some group of mates the chants resuming,
Ever with pleas'd smile I may keep on,
Ever and ever yet the verses owning—as first, I here and now,
Signing for soul and body, set to them my name.

Surely must we think that this Phèdre of Sarah Bernhardt is a poem that she would keep on ever and ever owning, a chant to be resumed, a verse to be declaimed before fellow-artists, before Clairon and before Rachel. Surely we must think of these late performances as the postscripts and codicils of a masterpiece conceived and perfected long ago.

Buzz, Buzz !

Madame Bernhardt's last appearance in *Phèdre* in England was in 1915.   It seemed inconceivable that the great line :

C'est Vénus toute entière à sa proie attachée

had ever been given with a finer frenzy of self-loathing and denunciation, of expiatory tearing at the victim's own flanks.   We may safely say that as long as she lives the actress will never lose that wonderful change in the middle of the line from ecstatic horror to bruised resignation.   It is possible that the long confessions to Œnone and the declaration to Hippolyte may not have quite the old physical energy ;   in the spirit these cataracts break as ragingly and as perilously as ever.   What the performance has gained with years is the determination of the artist to add one last perfection while it is yet day.   Never is the artist satisfied that the moment has come when the hands shall be folded and the finished work contemplated. The artist is in eternal pursuit of a term which he must never overtake ;   he lags half-willingly behind, straining after the one more perfection, the last late glimpse of new beauty.   So Sarah Bernhardt with Phèdre.   The power that was hers at her zenith she can never now exceed, may not always reproduce.   Her step may not always be as firm nor her eye as bright.   But those are the affairs of the body ;   Mme. Bernhardt has knowledge of the things that belong to the spirit, the things that o'ercrow and make a servant of the body, though

108

in the actor they must shine through the body.
And so it comes about that as time goes on, whatever there is less of the volcanic and cataclysmal
in this wonderful performance is more than com-
pensated by a rarer wistfulness, a more child-like
purity, an increasing pity.   More clearly than ever
this actress now declares her Phèdre the sport and
victim of the Immortals, the pure soul whipped
to impurity by the pitiless Goddess.   The vice of
Phèdre is, in Clairon's phrase, pure somnambulism,
and fatal and somnambulistic is the dry, brassy
horror of Sarah Bernhardt's passion.   The waking
of Phèdre, in which the poem attains to the limpidity
of spring mornings and the verse to a pure Mozartian
tinkle, shows her as a child who, unlashed by the
cruel goddess, only wanted to be " good."   This,
as Bernhardt does it, is pure exquisitiveness.   It is
the perfect postscript.   The actress puts into a
frigid figure of classic tragedy all human pathos
and pitifulness ; she brings this cold heroine home
to us even as she does her Frou - Frou and her
Marguerite.   " Pauvre Frou - Frou " is natural
enough ; that we should say " Pauvre Phèdre " is
astounding.   But then surely this Phèdre of Sarah
Bernhardt is the art of acting's last attainment.
" Là finit notre art sur terre " might fitly be applied
to a performance wonderful enough in plain fact,
most wonderful to those whose eyes can peer into
the eyes of the soul, whose ears are attentive to the
voice of the spirit.

Buzz, Buzz !

.　　.　　.　　.　　.　　.　　.

The art of Sarah Bernhardt has been subject to a thousand comparisons, to a summer's day, to tropical lightning, to a wild beast ravening upon prey, and by one gifted writer to four such dissimilar things as the view of Florence from Fiesole, a pheasant's neck, Leonardo's " Monna Lisa," and ripe corn with poppies in it. The mere apprehension of her acting has been said to produce " an obscure sensation of peril, such as one feels when the lioness leaps into the cage, on the other side of the bars." The animal and vegetable kingdoms have been ransacked for comparison that should be adequate, and the phrase-mongers have not been satisfied. None, it has been said, is a greater bore than he who insists upon describing one art in the terms of another, thinking to translate music into paint with a picture of St. Cecilia " in full blast at one of her own compositions ! " Admitted that it is a tedious and thankless task to translate fine acting into fine phrases. Those who have never seen Bernhardt will wonder at the tiresome excess of her critics' raptures ; those who remember her acting at its best will marvel at the panegyrist's ineffectual poverty.

I remember a glimpse of Sarah Bernhardt in her dressing-room at the Coliseum after a performance of some insignificant playlet of the war. In front of her glass, physically exhausted, but ever so mentally alert, sits the great craftswoman. Dis-

Sarah Bernhardt

dainful of subterfuge she gives you the full face of
which the lineaments belong to a nation, confronting
you unshrinkingly that you may read according to
your wit that mask on which a thousand passions
of the scene have left their trace.   She stretches
out the fine hand of the ageing artist, that hand
which so many tragic kings " have lipped and
trembled kissing."   The voice is hoarse now, but
in the restless eyes old fires smoulder.   The nostrils
are still aquiver, as who should say a horse scenting
peril.   The spirit is dauntless, defiant of age and
natural shock.   " Jusqu'au bout ! " the play's last
word of exhortation to France, might well be the
spiritual motto of the actress in her long and stern
fight against bodily distress.   " Quand-même ! "
her actual device, is the watchword of the steel
conscious and defiant of the fraying scabbard.

" Of what we call acting," says Arthur Symons
writing about her somewhere, " there is little, little
change in the expression of the face.   The part is
a part for the voice. . . ."   This was written of
Phèdre, but it is true of all her parts.   The passion
of Phèdre, the glory of Jeanne d'Arc, the glamour of
a Marguerite Gauthier are all so many solos for the
voice.   Personality is merged in a single effulgence
of which the penalty is to debar the actress from all
but the greatest creations.   Sarah Bernhardt may no
longer cope with the insignificant.   When she essays
the dying stripling of her war-play it may safely be said
that no actress could look less like a soldier wounded
on the field of battle.   But we must say in the same

Buzz, Buzz !

breath that no other living actress is capable of the wistful fingering of the standard, the flame of worship for the relic, the mystic delirium.

As one left the theatre one's mind went back to the first rising on a youthful horizon of this now setting star. From some untravelled end of the earth she had come, the wings of her genius gilding cities as she passed. To a child it was all very wonderful and incomprehensible, the long, pale posters in mauve and silver, the wait outside the theatre on a hot summer evening, the flushed and hectic play contrasting with the lingering red of the sunset, the ineffable acting, the unending recalls, the infinite grace of their acceptance, the taking out of the horses from the carriage, the suspension of human judgment on a player of such unreckonable mettle. This early enthusiasm can at the time have been little more than the early response to the exotic. One looks back, oh, ever so leniently, upon that half-discerning wonder which time has deepened so immeasurably. This art, which in its hey-day lit up a firmament, moves towards its setting in infinite serenity. We find a reason now for the old unreason ; incalculable glamour begins to fade. There has succeeded a lasting reverence for supreme workmanship, the enduring recognition of a great spirit.

Réjane

WHAT sojourner in the provinces would dream that his darkness could be changed to light by so radiant a star as Réjane ? What if the paltriness and absurdity of the playlet enshrining the great actress incline one to feel like some watcher of the skies who should have no greater marvel for observation than a smoky chimney ? It is a great thing to be put into touch once again with the great players of the world. Réjane may claim to be a citizen of whatever capital she pleases, though it is Paris which she trails more particularly at her heels. Not necessarily the modish city of *La Parisienne*, but the Paris of her earlier years, of the Porte Saint-Martin and the Place du Château d'Eau. Her art bears the marks of an apprenticeship that began in infancy. Not for nothing can an actress look back upon a childhood at the old Ambigu Theatre, have watched the funeral of Aimée Désclée and received the encouragements of a Barbey d'Aurevilly. Barbey thought her lithe as an adder ; Sarcey half-deplored her " petite frimousse éveillée," her air too wide-awake for the house of Molière. That suppleness to which Barbey alluded has passed into the wit and temper of the great comédienne ; the " too malicious countenance " of Sarcey has become the face a little disillusioned and a little tired of Sapho.

We lack a painter who shall show us, after the manner of Sir Joshua, the figure of Réjane torn between comedy and tragedy, now leaning to those middle-class adventurers which have enabled us to

Buzz, Buzz !

visualise Emma Bovary, Valérie Marneffe, and our own Becky Sharp, now yielding to the flick of raw human passion, animal affection, brute hate, and inarticulate suffering which gave us Germinie Lacerteux and the woman in *La Robe Rouge*. Réjane can do tragedy, or perhaps it would be better to say that she can do passionately in tragic things., For in this actress the serenity, aloofness, and repose that should go with tragic acting are absent ; lacking also the feeling for beauty in voice, manner, and movement. In compensation there is the blazing and overwhelming temperament and the technical facility. The hoarse voice, which can be as stirring as any sweetness long drawn out, the mask of infinite challenge and provocation, the air of perfect *blague*, of tolerance and unshocked knowledge of life—these are the traits we look for in Réjane. Her creatures are proper as Beatrice and Portia are proper ; that is to say, that they have faced life frankly and found it good. Their presentation may stir or frighten or amaze, but you may be sure of this, that ever and always the characters of Réjane will be found to bear the hallmark of the woman of the world. There is justification and to spare for the gibe with which, in the playlet, the actress is made to flout the Prussian officer : " Talk of Kultur, and never heard of Réjane ! "

Laurence Irving

A RARE, curious creature. One saw him as a young man, the finest Justice Shallow of this or any age. One saw him later in a drama—*Theresa*, I think it was called—that ran three nights, in which he was very busy with pistols and poisons. Then one lost sight of him or heard of him only in the provinces with plays of little renown, among them a *Lovelace* of his own contriving, if I remember aright. Then a queer play called *Typhoon*, in which multitudinous Japs strove for precedence in hanging and Irving went to enormous pains to give his nervous and expressive features the proper cast of immobility. Some little time before his tragic death he appeared in *Hamlet*. It was the only time since his appearance as a very young man in the *Second Part of King Henry IV.* that I had seen him in a play worthy of his genius. Since recollection does not better what I wrote then, I reproduce it here.

What are we to think of this new Hamlet— curious, sinister, faulty, rare ; of a presentation of the play in which the soliloquy " To be or not to be " and the " Get-thee-to-a-nunnery " scene precede the speech " O, what a rogue, etc." ? Well it would really seem that when a first-class dramatist has first-class stuff to say it matters very little in what order he says it, and certainly no violence was done last night to the coherence of the play. What does matter, since it must have a very intimate and important bearing upon the actor, is the restoration

Buzz, Buzz !

of the feverish incidents that follow Hamlet's departure from his mother's closet. These never-acted scenes are the very ecstasy of nightmare, a projection of the horrid phantoms trafficking in Hamlet's brain. Perhaps in this picture of over-wrought nerves Shakespeare did actually achieve the writing for all time with which he is so handsomely and carelessly credited. In these scenes the poet may be said to bridge over that little fraction of time which separates our century from his. Hamlet's mad tricks with the body of Polonius, his petulant hiding of it, the courtiers' nagging quest of it are close enough to our time to provoke even so modern a burlesque as *Sumurûn*, with Rosencrantz and Guildenstern for hideous clown and loon. That *macabre* conversation beginning " A certain con-vocation of politic worms are e'en at him " might be Villiers de l'Isle Adam, or any of the Frenchmen ; the mania for an exact apportioning of the blame between " Bestial oblivion or some craven scruple of thinking too precisely on the event " is sheer Baudelaire in its sickness.

One realised that of all our moderns Mr. Laurence Irving, with his strangely sinister temper, could best afford the restoration of these scenes. Mr. Forbes-Robertson's exquisite sentimentalist, that paragon of tenderness to be worn in our heart's core, " ay, in our heart of hearts," is not all Hamlet. Mr. Benson's gnarled, tortured, twisted figure of the Dane, sheer botching 'prentice-work as a credible *imitation* of humanity, yet inspiring as a gargoyle, is nearer the proper dæmonic fury. But not even this is all Hamlet. The actor who shall give us these restored scenes must come to grips with intellectual danger, the insistent toying with an idea of wantonness, the artist's loving elaboration of that frailty which, once played with and " placed " in his imagination, he is most urgent to condemn. Hamlet has the courage of the perilous stuff of which the brave thinker, for sheer interest's sake, would not wish his bosom too well cleansed. The sinister itch, the spleen that finds its images in a sun breeding maggots in a dead dog, and its most exquisite sensation in the doom of all living flesh—" and now my Lady Worm's,"—this instinct for rottenness and death—" your worm is your only emperor for diet "—is as much a part of Hamlet, whether we like it or not, as the most urbane of his philosophy, the most flower-like of his chivalry, the last of his tenderness. These extreme reconciliations are the difficulty of Hamlet. The actor may well cry out with Macbeth, " Who can be wise, amazed, temperate, and furious ? "—vital and decadent, he might add ; and to place a Hamlet is almost inevitably to determine the measure of the compromise.

Mr. Irving's compromise takes the form of a wholesale discarding of all the tenderness and grace that is the foundation of the " sweet prince " of Horatio's epitaph and of our imaginations. Superficially this would seem to be an intolerable Hamlet. Mr. Irving has no poetry, his soliloquies breathe scant philosophy, his passion for Ophelia is perfunctory, his upbraiding of the Queen mere black-guarding. The actor has little pathos ; not once did he move us in any purely human way. The voice is apparently beyond control ; gusts of sound blow out the phrases like bellying sails, piping treble and bo'sun's bass are indifferent in meaning ; wrong stresses are thick as leaves in Vallombrosa. Mr. Irving will say, " And by a sleep to say we end," and come entirely to a full stop. Then, after a long pause, we get the disjointed and now meaningless, " The heartache and the thousand natural shocks." This is only one of a score of instances. And yet —and yet we think this is a great and finely imaginative Hamlet. These twists and torturings become a quality. This Hamlet is an overgrown child, a cuffed and cowed schoolboy misunderstood by his schoolfellow, the world ; he is an animal, in-articulate in suffering, a cub if you like, coltish certainly. He does not grow up, he goes over to some sickly creature of Huysmans or Baudelaire. His voice, we want to say, has the break of im-maturity. One is conscious that this praise of an actor's defects is not generally considered fair criti-cism, however the defects may fit with our better appreciation. No lucky correspondence with a spectator's mood can justify such diction as Mr. Irving's. Rather we must find justification for this fine Hamlet in its blaze of romantic energy, its white-heat of conception, its terror, dignity, austerity. We had the old fascination of watching a towering intellect playing with little minds ; there was the

118

Laurence Irving

romantic figure and rich expressive gesture ; there
was the sense of power and the feeling that, inevitably and with all its faults, this was a fine
thing.

Sir Johnston Forbes-Robertson

It was on a spring evening in 1917 that I saw Forbes-Robertson. I was due to return to the south of France on the following day, and could find nothing more typically English for my last night of leave than Mr. Jerome's *Passing of the Third Floor Back*. There is something sad in the decadence of an actor, in a last cessation from soaring, a late acquiescence in mediocrity, a life's end consent to the commonplace. Sir Johnston Forbes-Robertson may have pleaded with himself that charity is a greater thing than art and in time of war should prevail.[1] But it was a sad thing to see this gracious and noble actor come back to the stage as the transfigurer of rubbish. Many years ago this actor's appearance as the Launcelot of some Arthurian play—gallant alike in sage-green doublet and in bearing—was deemed by so unhysterical a playgoer as Mr. Bernard Shaw to be a picture too radiant for mortal eyes. What a fall is there to the Galahad of Mr. Jerome! A Galahad in broadcloth, too, bound with a decent ribbon. The hat is shapeless and the trousers baggy with excess of genuflexion. The whole, oh, so indescribably common!

" Do you think," says one of the boarders with reference to the mysterious lodger, " do you think he is quite a gentleman ? " and an appreciative little snigger runs through the house, in no doubt

[1] Throughout the revival of Mr. Jerome's play the services of Sir Johnston Forbes-Robertson and of all the members of his company were given without remuneration in aid of War Charities.

Sir Johnston Forbes-Robertson

on the genteel score, since the Stranger took the
tray out of the hands of the little serving-maid.
The fact that the girl has been in the habit of lifting
trays ever since she went out to service and that
the offer must be offensive to the girl's mistress
does not weigh with your popular audience. Quite
the gentleman ! would be the unanimous verdict,
opposition quailing at the imminent prospect of a
stoning to death in Northumberland Avenue at
the hands of the Stranger's outraged disciples.
One naturally hesitates to declare the practice of
Christian precept to be a purely middle-class virtue.
Yet the only alternative would seem to be the
admission of certain essential disqualifications implicit in good breeding. Just as your thoroughbred will not take kindly to leather, so humanity's
high-steppers would seem to scorn the collar and
traces of humility. It is significant that the chival-
rous knight who would relieve servant girls of their
platters is rarely to be met with in the pages of our
fastidious writers. But this is by the way.

For those who did not pay too great attention
to the play, the evening in the little theatre at
Charing Cross must have been crowded with old
recollection. With memories of a lean and noble
Othello, of a finely-tempered Shylock, of a Hamlet
distillable into the single phrase of Horatio : " Good-
night, sweet prince." With memories, too, of a
hundred graceful gentlemen, guileless fools, if you
will, but not the other-worldly simpleton around
whose shoulders Mr. Jerome has endeavoured to

Buzz, Buzz !

cast the mantle of—to look no higher—Dostoievsky's
Idiot. This mysterious and semi-reverend Personage must be considered as belonging to the actor's
less successful gallery of lounge-suited, bowler-
hatted heroes. Sir Johnston Forbes-Robertson
has always cut too mediæval a figure for serge,
his brow was always too yonderly for the latest
fashion in felt. Strange that this actor has only
to don a morning-coat to effect a descent into
the commonplace ! His Dick in Mr. Kipling's
The Light that Failed was instinct with the touch of
the hair-dresser, although one failed to put a finger
on the doubtful gesture or faulty intonation. In
Mr. Jerome's play the embodiment of a benign
austerity is turned lay-preacher. With this author
at the stops, the grand organ which is Forbes-
Robertson's voice attunes itself to the unctuous
droning of the smaller decencies and the more
trivial commandments. And yet, as the final exit,
the tawdry apotheosis, the reverences of the serving-
maid drew to their unconscionable close, one forgave
the actor.

For it is not by a Mysterious Stranger that
Sir Johnston Forbes-Robertson will be ultimately
judged. He goes down to history as the most
popular Hamlet since Henry Irving,—popular in
the non-detrimental sense of appealing most nearly
to the general sympathy. The elder Dumas in a
well-known passage says of Othello that the part
used to be played " by Talma with his art, Kean
with his temperament, Kemble with his mastery

Sir Johnston Forbes-Robertson

of all that the traditions of the stage could do for him, Macready with his physical beauty, Joanny with his instincts." Of Forbes-Robertson we may say that he played Hamlet with careful and patient art, the temperament of an English gentleman— Meredith's Sir Willoughby would have played him so—and the lustre and distinction of what had once been great physical beauty. This Hamlet had not the interest of Laurence Irving's tortuous and greatly daring venture nor the garish excellence of his brother's admirable piece of showmanship. But it was unmatched, we must think, in our time for serenity and steadfastness and high aloofness from the encroaching spirit of compromise. It was the Hamlet on which the mind dwells most lovingly. To many of us perhaps he was the " sweet prince " *tout court* without need for preamble or elaboration.

It is perhaps necessary to define exactly what we mean when we say that an actor is or is not Hamlet. Mr. Walkley has an admirable passage [1] on this subject :

A real person is the resultant of his will, hereditary circumstances, environment, and millions of causes entirely beyond his control. A dramatist's personage is a mere projection of one man's mind, limited by his powers of observation and imagination, something vague that has been held in solution in the dramatist's consciousness until it is "precipitated" in the form of words written upon paper. It is, as the mathematicians say, a mere " function " of the

---

[1] *Drama and Life*, chapter entitled " Professor Bradley's *Hamlet*."

Buzz, Buzz !

dramatist, and can utter nothing, think nothing, be nothing outside the range of the dramatist's own nature and mental vision. Now the confusion between the "historic" and the "dramatic" personage is natural enough. The whole art of fiction, particularly the art of drama, with its flesh-and-blood materials, is based upon the possibility of producing this confusion in the reader's or spectator's mind. The confusion gives pleasure, for we seem, by yielding to it, to be witnessing a veritable act of creation and to be enlarging, enriching, vividly colouring our experience of life. . . . And so if we want to understand the play of *Hamlet*, we shall not do so by assuming that it is a piece of real life, lived by people who have independent lives outside it. We can only hope to understand it by starting with the simple common-place truth that it is a work of art contrived by a certain man at a certain time under certain influences and with certain objects. I should apologise for expatiating on the obvious were it not that the old fallacy, the old confusion between reality and art, is still to be met with among our foremost Shakespearian critics. The reason, no doubt, is that, as Morgann put it, Shakespeare is so much greater than the other men that he seems to be different in kind, and not merely in degree—whereas, of course, he is not different in kind, and it is hopelessly uncritical to assume that he works under different conditions from those of other playwrights merely because he does so much better than they do.

So far so good. But Mr. Walkley goes on to maintain that Hamlet was endowed with charm of character solely because his author wanted a "sympathetic" hero ; with a love of acting—to account for the play-scene ; with a love of fencing —to enable him to polish off his step-father at the long last. Mr. Walkley declares for a Hamlet sane

124

Sir Johnston Forbes-Robertson

as a County Court Judge, but feigning more than the proverbial hatter's madness :

Might one suggest that Shakespeare, fond, like all the Elizabethan dramatists, of madness as a dramatic *motif*, meant to have " mad scenes " for Hamlet at any cost; that as he also wanted him for sane actions and speeches, the madness had to be feigned; and that nevertheless, when the madness *motif* was being treated on the stage, Shakespeare (as was the custom of his theatre) treated it " for all it was worth," careless of the boundaries between feigning and reality ?

Admirable ! And again :

Professor Bradley would ascribe Hamlet's characteristics to some precedent *état d'âme* in Hamlet himself. I would ascribe them to the fact that Shakespeare himself had these characteristics, and sought expression for them on the stage without a perpetual solicitude for consistency or intelligibility of character in his mouthpiece.

Excellent, i'faith ! So excellent that it involves us in two tremendous difficulties. First, that we are to take Shakespeare, through his own fault or the fault of his time, for a less skilful story-teller than, say, Dickens. Second, that Hamlet becomes from the actor's point of view sovereignly unplayable.

To take these stumbling-blocks in their order. The whole art of fiction, we echo, is based upon producing in the reader's mind confusion between the " historic " and " dramatic " personage. Dickens achieved this confusion to perfection. Micawber is life itself. There is nothing for which the reader is unprepared in his exit of monumental despair

125

Buzz, Buzz !

and his cheerful reappearance on the top of the Canterbury coach in company with a bottle and a bag of shrimps. We *know* Micawber. He has *lived* the intervening interval. We can account for him when he is not on the stage. In the same way we know what Joe Gargery was doing and dreaming and " meantersay "-ing through all the years of Pip's neglect. We can account for him too. Are we to account in a lesser degree for Hamlet ? Are we to enter into elaborate discussion as to whether his author was unable to rid himself of the shackles of his form, since he must needs adapt character to the exigencies of plot ? Or shall we think that he was merely careless of the plausibilities ? [1] There is no way out of the dilemma. Either we must find for a consistent Hamlet, difficult, curious, " modern," if you like, but alive and to be accounted for, or we must reduce him to a mere bagful of histrionics. (Mr. Shaw has persistently said much the same thing and been soundly rated for his outspokenness.)

For the actor the choice is all-important. That is to say, that he has no choice. His not to reason about Hamlet, but to play him as a creature of flesh and blood, capable of arousing and holding our

---

[1] The poet gives other hints besides the obvious one of Polonius that he is supremely capable of such a disregard. We declare poetry, for instance, to be ingrained in Macbeth and then we come upon Banquo in the same vein.

> There's husbandry in heaven ;
> Their candles are all out,

says this very secondary personage. The mouth is Banquo's but the voice belongs to Shakespeare.

Sir Johnston Forbes-Robertson

sympathies. No audience has ever yet assembled which we can fob off with Mr. Walkley's version of Hamlet as programme music with " A Father's Advice to his Son " or " The Art of Acting " or " Meditations on Suicide " for themes. There are two ways in which the actor may nail his Hamlet to the boards. If he be of the stupendous order he may risk the whole of him, incomprehensibilities and all ; if his genius be of gentler mould, he may cleave the Prince in twain and throw away what is from his point of view decidedly the worser part. We may take the first to have been the great Kean's way and the way of any other immoderate virtuoso. We may take it that they got over Shakespeare's carelessness in treating the madness *motif* for all it was worth by treating it for all *they* were worth. Not so much the lightning-flash as the thunder-roll. The actor of the old bombastical school may be said to have bluffed his audience, throwing off the big soliloquies as the hero of the concert-platform throws off his cadenza, settling down again after the hand-clapping to the sober business of his original Concerto. So the great actor in *Hamlet*, the out-of-gear and the stark incredible delivered with such magnificence as to stagger understanding. The old actors believed in interpretation by force of terror. They frightened their heroes, if not into perception, at least into acquiescence.

But this is not the modern way and it was not Sir Johnston Forbes-Robertson's. The " book of words " or acting version proffered on entering the

Buzz, Buzz !

theatre was made up of all that there is in the play
of the gentle and the seemly. Since something
must be left out, it were well to leave out the un-
governable, we may imagine the actor postulating.
Therefore must this Hamlet lock within his bosom
the turgid, warped, and perilous stuff which, says
Mr. Walkley, is not Hamlet but Shakespeare.
Therefore must he shed his grosser metaphors
and hide that Rabelaisian cast of mind which, says
the critic, is not the Prince of Denmark but his
author. For this reason the Queen shall be reasoned
with, not bullied. It were well, too, to shear of their
ghoulishness the hero's pranks with the body of
Polonius :

> I'll lug the guts into the neighbour room,

and

> You shall nose him as you go upstairs into the lobby,

are unthinkable in the mouth of this Hamlet. The
actor, lacking the power to make the spectator's
heart knock at his ribs, will elect subconsciously
for a Hamlet which shall make no such demands.
Therefore was Sir Johnston Forbes-Robertson's
Hamlet the sanest individual at Court and the
least given to hysteria. The actor contrived the
whole of the Get-thee-to-a-nunnery scene in exactly
the same spirit in which David Garrick in the play
of that name simulates drunkenness, that is, for the
benefit of the spectators, in this case, eavesdroppers.
There was even less of self-pity in this Dane than in
the strolling actor. Here the reader may say that

128

Sir Johnston Forbes-Robertson

this is not Hamlet at all, but a shell, an abstraction, a residuum.

And such, in sooth, it was—a clarification of pure exquisiteness. This was the Hamlet catalogued by Ophelia, the courtier, soldier, scholar, the " expectancy and rose of the fair state." It was above all the Hamlet of natural feeling. This was a son whose affection for his murdered father was *real*—the best that most Hamlets achieve in this line being the perfunctory reverence of the Chinaman. This was a son who refrained from putting into the scene with his mother the insolence and bravado proper to Hamlets of commoner mould. " On ne doit jamais être grossier envers sa mère," said Sarah Bernhardt, speaking approvingly of Forbes-Robertson's exquisite conduct of this scene. But all the natural feelings of the man were wonderfully well done. The filial compassion of :

> And when you are desirous to be blessed,
> I'll blessing beg of you ;

and the tender homage to his friend :

> Give me that man
> That is not passion's slave, and I will wear him
> In my heart's core, ay, in my heart of heart,
> As I do thee,

were the most beautifully delivered lines in the play. Nor was the esteem for Laertes lacking. This Hamlet jumped into the grave offended in the dilettante's punctilious sense of offence by the

" bravery " of the other's grief, as he is careful to
explain later on, and not in a fit of hysterical over-
weeningness.   Passion in all its forms was abhorrent
to him ; to the Arthurian temperament he added
warmth of heart and the imagination of a boundless
charity.   His measureless force of moral indignation
was without priggishness.   He would handle the
vices and follies of mankind as curiously as he
handled the jester's skull, wiping away the dust of
contact with the same nicety of disdain :

> Let the bloat king tempt you again to bed ;
> Pinch wanton on your cheek ; call you his mouse ;
> And let him, for a pair of reechy kisses,
> Or paddling in your neck with his damn'd fingers . . .

was the very whip and scourge of lechery.

I have said that Forbes-Robertson played the
part with his physical grace.   I should have added
mental graciousness.   It is impossible to describe
the winning sweetness of this kindly Hamlet, his
grave courtesy in rebuke.   When he listened his
whole soul seemed to go out to meet the other's
words.   He conceived baseness and treachery with
difficulty, though he would inveigh mightily against
them.   " Can these things be ? " he would be
saying, strong in his own purged sense of integrity
and honour.   He had also what I should like to
call a peculiarly English sense of self-control and
the decencies of soliloquy.   To a Mounet-Sully or
a Salvini, " Bloody, bawdy villain !   Remorseless,
treacherous, lecherous, kindless villain ! " would

Sir Johnston Forbes-Robertson

be merely the small change of vituperation, rendering the ensuing lines meaningless. To Forbes-Robertson's Hamlet this was mere brawling exceeding the modesty of nature, and his severest contempt was reserved for himself that he must, like a whore, unpack his heart with words. It was a Hamlet not without humour, but equally without hint of the *macabre*. It was a kindly, ironical, astringent humour such as Elia would have loved, enabling him to live in the clouds and descend to earth upon occasion. " This most excellent canopy," he would say, and then, remembering that he is talking to Guildenstern, add in explanatory fashion, " the air, look you."

In point of decorative beauty this Hamlet exceeded calculation. Every movement across the stage, every lift of the hand was a sheer delight to the eye, the voice so resonant and so noble as to deserve Hamlet's own epithet of " miraculous organ." I have already said of the whole character that it was distillable into the single phrase " Sweet prince." Not the whole of the poet's creation, if you will ; but the most that may be given by an actor who seeks to touch, without puzzling, our profoundest sympathies.

Mrs. Patrick Campbell

My first recollection of this brilliant actress is in an English version of *Fédora* at the Haymarket Theatre. I suppose this must have been at some time in the late 'eighties. I was not a very experienced playgoer, and I remember my chief impression to have been one of amazement that the death-like pallor of Fédora in her last moments should come off on the sleeve of the actor who was then plain Mr. H. Beerbohm Tree. In the early 'nineties Fame was very busy with Mrs. Patrick Campbell. Eager and excited playgoers mewed up in the provinces—how many thousands of us were there, I wonder?—were getting ready to welcome the new celebrity over whom the London journals enthused so immoderately. Then suddenly—in October 1893, to be exact—the famous actress burst upon the provincial darkness in *The Second Mrs. Tanqueray*. About this performance a great provincial critic, the late W. T. Arnold, contented himself with saying: " The interest of the performance centres, of course, in Mrs. Patrick Campbell's Paula. It is a character-study of extraordinary fascination, and puts the actress into the front rank of her profession. It was as good in the charming little love scene between her and Aubrey in the first act as in the great scenes with Ellean and Captain Ardale. Her courage and frankness are admirably conveyed, and not less so the steps of the transformation by which she is gradually converted from a selfish woman, greedy for pleasure and excitement, into a loving and suffering one."

132

Mrs. Patrick Campbell

Take in conjunction with this description of Mrs. Campbell's acting another sentence in the same notice of this very learned and admirable critic : " She (Paula) is also an inexorable little realist "— and we realise that the two together give but a poor account of the actress. " Little " is the last epithet to be applied to Paula as portrayed by Mrs. Patrick Campbell.

This is not the time of day for an exhaustive analysis of an antiquated play, memorable enough in its period, nor yet for a detailed criticism of a piece of acting which has passed into the history of the English stage. I go back to Paula as the first of a long line of parts—Magda, Agnes Ebbsmith, the wife or mistress in *Es Lebe das Leben*—of which the prevailing note was one of overpowering luxury and magnificence. It seemed as though we were at last to have a star of our own, a luminary not too palpably outshone by French and Italian genius. It is true that we still had Ellen Terry, but that dear and great lady was too firmly embedded in all our hearts to be capable of the quality of amazement. There were a few good and one or two great artists in the country, but they were chiefly occupied in interpreting Ibsen and Mr. Shaw at unfashionable hours in places difficult to find. Mrs. Campbell, on the other hand, stood for all a poet of the period—who was really no poet at all but a draughtsman, one Beardsley, to wit—meant by

réclame and recall,
Paris and St. Petersburg, Vienna and St. James's Hall.

Buzz, Buzz !

" I like fruit when it's expensive," says Paula in one of her outbursts of frank vulgarity, and the theatre-goer is not yet born who can resist portrayal on the stage of the seamy and expensively seamy side of life. Mrs. Campbell's parts about this time shone with a factitious but very splendid magnificence. Paula, wearing the sumptuous livery of the *déclassé*, Magda hardly less gorgeously arrayed, even the socialistic Agnes unbaring her shoulders for the delectation of Lucas Cleeve, were all more or less " sympathetic " heroines whose troubles arose from having " burst Joy's grape " against their palate more or less fine. They were exactly the sort of heroine that foreign and cometary genius delights to travel from one end of the habitable globe to the other.

But in and among these sophistications were other portraits of a different order — Mariana, Ophelia, Mélisande. The first was a hyper-civilised and romantical creature of Echegaray. The play is dim in my memory. All I remember is Mariana's recital of being snatched up in her mother's arms to the lover's urging of " Be quick ! Be quick ! " It was in this scene that Mrs. Campbell first struck for me what was afterwards to be her note, the note of extravagant importunacy, of pleading for more than life can hold, of childish mutiny, of animal distress. All of which would appear to be a matter of intonation of the voice and a way of turning the head to give the wonderful sweep of throat and chin. These the means ; all praise to the artist who could make such sovereign use of them.

Ophelia and Mélisande go together, though widely separate in point of time. I forget to whose Hamlet the Ophelia, probably Sir Herbert Tree's ; the Pelléas was, of course, Sarah Bernhardt. Both characters had the same fragility of intellect. They moved on the borderland of something we may call the spirit-world, a kinder term than lunacy. (Shakespeare showed a fine tact in not overburthening his moody Dane. Add a love-affair of real poignancy to his other troubles, *ce serait trop fort.* Ophelia glides in and out of the play with the least of dynamic disturbance. Almost we may say that *Hamlet* without the young lady would still be playable.) Mrs. Campbell was perfection in the part ; her madness nothing more than the jangling of bells out of tune, a straying rather than a positive disorder of the senses. Her Mélisande was a child, but a child holding its own with her great lover. I do not mean to imply that the two performances deserved an equal number of marks, but simply that the world at that time contained no other mate for such a Pelléas.

It is this quality of childish rebellion against Fate which made the success of those other Paulas and Magdas. They were not mere women of the world, butterflies to be broken after their little hour. They were women of whom it could truly be said, as was never quite the case with Bernhardt's pathetical *courtisane,* " Quoi que l'on soit devenue, on a toujours eu une enfance."

Buzz, Buzz!

I have left to the last what was perhaps Mrs. Campbell's most amazing performance,—her Hedda Gabler. For my part I found it a wonderful piece of acting to look upon, listen to, and think over. It was acting for the eyes and ears. It made Hedda a creature of iridescence, a-moral and imperious. Those who understand Hedda *à fond* tell me that the actress made the right points and none but the right points in exactly the right way. I remember being perfectly " convinced " at the time, without being able to find the right words in which to express conviction. But then not even Mr. William Archer has been able to find exactly the right words in which to explain the character to us—not even in Norwegian. It was a performance which I would willingly go ten times to see. But that is the way with great players. They give you so very little of their very best.

The last time I saw Mrs. Patrick Campbell was on the stage of a London music-hall, in some playlet of the desert. I am afraid I did not pay a great deal of attention. It all seemed to be so very like a bad dream. . . .

Sir F. R. Benson

Two portraits I select out of this actor's gallery, the
spare and meagre Don of Cervantes and the lean
Antony of Shakespeare. The elder Irving—and
it is curious how all the paths of austerity lead back
to our great actor—was, of course, the ideal Don
Quixote of this or any other century. We can see
him, beautiful in tight armour, his soul " divinely
loose about him," as Herbert has it, poring over
the pages of *Amadis de Gaula*. And we cannot
imagine that grave gentleman tumbling on the
ground, head downward, buttocks aloft, as did Sir
F. R. Benson in the part. But this is the very spirit
in which the younger actor has always revelled, in
which he has so often tackled Shakespeare. His
playing of the Don in I forget what particular
adaptation was conceived in a composite vein of
Elizabethan clowning and the *esprit gaulois*, was
magnificently suited to that colossal monument of
blague, out of which the portrait of the knight shyly
peers like some cathedral window among gargoyles.
The actor is free of the great spirit of all time ; he
has lived with the great plays and we feel his large
and healthy sympathy with the book written in
prisons and taverns and on the open highway.
What have been called faults help him enormously
with the Don. His body is often all at posing,
the management of his hands ungainly and such as
the meanest ballet-dancer would scorn, his voice
untutored, blowing where it listeth, now plumbing,
now soaring, often at odds with plain and sober

meaning. And yet he will strike an attitude—Richard's in prison with his leg drawn up under his chin—that will remain with you always ; his hands will eke out a phrase, his voice become a full-stringed instrument, a gust of speech, a wind tearing the ragged cloud of some doubtful passage and giving you a glimpse of blue. Cervantes' humour sweeps like a vigorous breeze over malodorous places at which a more squeamish latter-day public is constrained to hold its nose. The modern play speaks with a " snaffling voyce." Sir F. R. Benson's wilful uglinesses and the tart, rough quality of his acting restore much of the bite and tang lost in the text of any practicable adaptation.

All the world lovès a lover, and it is curious that Sir Frank has not taken more kindly to the playing of them. For surely that rare uncouthness of his, that awkward grace, make him if not the most exquisite certainly the most interesting and least insipid lover on the English stage. We might cite Orlando as the type of devout, single-minded young lover which Antony certainly was not. Our actor when he played Rosalind's lover used to graft on to that immature, tentative passion the quite unusual interest of an older and more expert lover's playing for position. Now mark him in *Antony and Cleopatra*, that perilous and royal gambit in passion with its eager elimination of preliminary fencing, its immediate challenging to the issue of " pure love." Note now how the actor spiritualises this frank soldier, how he gets the better of the

138

opening exchanges, how his fury of passion quite o'ertops the most extravagant of Cleopatra's caprice. Note how much of nobility still is left to this madman in the very extremity of his befoolment. Sir F. R. Benson, who will not put out his intellectual fires even for Caliban, is the finest of our actors for that side of Antony which is not the gross feeder and bluff man of the wars. For Antony must always be of Cleopatra's mettle, a lover worthy of all the passion and ruin of his great *débâcle* ; he is a Colossus undone and not a mere mountain of unconsidering valour. If there is anything intellectually more contemptible than gambling within one's means it is the throwing of world-stakes without proper appreciation of the splendour of the game. The fineness of Antony lies in his gambler's sense of style, his magnificently mannered throwing away of empire and reputation as though they were counters. You belittle Antony if you let him apprehend but carelessly the magnitude of his throws, if you deny him boding consciousness of ultimate bankruptcy. All this dignity and sense of style Sir F. R. Benson gets easily. With that tremendous force of personality, the actor could do little less. Yet there are times when Antony's fate gets too big even for Antony, and it is then that the part comes down to simplicities. All that outroaring of a bull of Bashan, that blind lowering and charging of a head bowed in bloody desperation, are the dumb animal outraged. Benson here scarcely gave the sense of a pitiless rain of blows

139

Buzz, Buzz !

bending the hardly corrigible neck.   There was a
trifle too much of subtlety in the suggestion of the
gathering clouds of retribution.   Towards the close
of the play Antony should stand in a vast and empty
plain like some lone leader of a hornéd herd tossing
his head to the storm.   Sheer resentment now,
past all analysis.   Mr. Louis Calvert used to be
magnificent with his sullens, his savagery, his
stoicism.   Sir F. R. Benson was all austerity and
fortitude.   Nor did we always get from him the
full-bloodedness of this great *viveur*, this gor-
mandiser.   This spare and fastidious Antony would
not have found, even for the Cleopatra of his reviling,
so gross and ogreish a simile as the " morsel, cold
upon dead Caesar's trencher."   " To-night I'll
make the wine peep through their stars " is the
rhapsody of a more generous temperament than this
lean Antony's, but " Call to me all my sad captains "
was most beautifully given.

Of all actors who flourished in my time, Bensley had
most of the swell of soul, was greatest in the delivery of
heroic conceptions, the emotions consequent upon the presentment of a great idea to the fancy.   He had the true
poetical enthusiasm—the rarest faculty among players.
None that I remember possessed even a portion of that
fine madness which he threw out in Hotspur's famous rant
about glory, or the transports of the Venetian incendiary at
the vision of the fired city.   His voice had the dissonance,
and at times the inspiring effect, of the trumpet.   His gait
was uncouth and stiff, but no way embarrassed by affectation ;
and the thoroughbred gentleman was uppermost in every
movement.   He seized the moment of passion with greatest

140

truth; like a faithful clock, never striking before the time; never anticipating or leading you to anticipate. He was totally destitute of trick and artifice. He seemed come upon the stage to do the poet's message simply, and he did it with as genuine fidelity as the nuncios in Homer deliver the errands of the gods. He let the passion or the sentiment do its own work without prop or bolstering. He would have scorned to mountebank it; and betrayed none of that *cleverness* which is the bane of serious acting.

Thus Lamb on Bensley, and for the first half I should be content to read the name of our own greatest Shakespearean actor. " Fine madness," " famous rant," " the dissonance of the trumpet," " the gait uncouth and stiff," the " thoroughbred gentleman "—all this is pure Benson—only it is not true of the later actor that he always strikes to time. I have seen Sir F. R. Benson blown about by gusts of passion when there was not wind stirring in the text to start a rustle among dry leaves; I have heard the actor strike midnight and high noon together on all the clocks, belfries, gongs, and alarums of his astounding vocal resources, when there was no urgency discoverable in the business in hand. For the rest of the comparison I can vouch—at least as to similarity of intention. Sir F. R. Benson is always pleased to let Shakespeare speak for himself *in so far as is practicable*; he will see to it that the voice of the poet shall at no time be interrupted nor the stream of the verse impeded. Does the actor forget his words? Then is a line snatched from another play, or the actor will pad the vacancy with some very burning Shakespeare-sounding matter of his own.

"There roared the sea, and trumpet-clangour sounds," said Pistol of the music at the coronation of King Henry. If he had said this of our tragedian's amazing vocal performances he would have been putting it mildly. The verse in *Antony and Cleopatra* is molten and brassy; Sir F. R. Benson puts into it the blare of trumpets, the clash of cymbals, the clang of opposing shields, and if some of the sounds do not always mean very much in themselves, their sum makes up the most astounding and inspiring symphony to be heard on the English stage to-day.

Henry Austin

GREAT acting may be measured by its power to haunt, and Henry Austin's Wiedemann [1] was a persistent obsession. All the more persistent in view of an inherent quality of shyness, making the performance a thing not to be advertised, ticketed for public admiration, but rather to be hugged to oneself as the painter in Henry James's story hugged his old lady, so unmistakably a " find," so curiously and beautifully " it." For Austin's Wiedemann, as beautifully " it " as Granger's Miss Wenham, was the dream performance of a dream theatre. It was full of the fine shades for which, on a palpable stage, one has ceased to hope ; half-turns of body to match half-turns of thought, vague fumbling of hands more explicit than spoken words, a vocabulary of infinitely graded expressiveness with which, despite the evidence of eyes and ears, you refused to credit the actor, so impossible did it seem that these things could be meant, or that the actor, having imagined them for his own delight, should still persist in the desperate task of getting them over footlights to a row of stalls. You felt that you alone in the house were being played to. But that was not it, for there was your neighbour, quite unwarrantably it seemed to you, under the same spell. Could it have been something in the tone of the voice, the manner of the walk ? But there again was not it, for one had heard the accent of pathos before, and admired a

[1] Sudermann's *Das Glück im Winckel*.

Buzz, Buzz !

sad and listless strut without the same intensity of satisfaction. Nor could one entirely assume a happy effect of personality, the luck of a part slipping on the actor like an old coat. One had caught glimpses of Wiedemann in others of Henry Austin's parts, but never before had there been this wonderful display of abandonment, annihilation, failure. There was in this old tutor something of the dazed animal's shake of the head, something of the broken nerve of a child and an infinity of gentleness. You were allowed to read what you liked into the performance ; it was there to be read into. And always when your reading was done there remained the exquisite *genre* picture of the German professor, full of what the painters call style. It was set back, put away from you, as it were, so that there was nothing of newness, of reality about it. The picture had almost what Henry James calls the " tone of time." It had ceased to be acting.[1]

[1] This is a figure of speech and the purest nonsense. I mean, of course, that it had begun by being, had continued to be, and had ended by being the very finest part of pure acting.

Miss Darragh[1]

SOME few years ago there was produced at one of our Repertory Theatres an admirable burlesque,[2] in which was offered up for sacrifice the whole crowd of "intellectuals"—playwright, producer, actor, and critic. In it there occurred the following lines :

Harrow (a tragedian). Do you mean to say I'm not a competent actor ?
Push (a manager). I should call you a Repertory actor.

The passage describes exactly what sort of a player Miss Darragh is not. Then let us recall the Repertory actor who, desponding of intellectual success, decided to "go back to the profession," and we have a clue to the kind of actress Miss Darragh decidedly is. She belongs, definitely, to "the profession"; she is able to do things on the stage, which is better, and always will be better, than thinking about them. I remember, in one of Mr. Galsworthy's plays, an actress going to the window and, with her back to the audience, flapping her arms up and down in the manner of one engaged in Swedish drill. Tactful questioning elicited the information that the movement (one, two, three, four ! *and* again, please!) was intended to represent the beat of wings, the soul's thrust for freedom. Delicate conception, grotesque performance ! This

---

[1] This article was written when Miss Darragh was still living and in the fulness of her powers.
[2] *Nothing like Leather,* by A. N. Monkhouse. Produced by Miss Horniman's Company at the Gaiety Theatre, Manchester, September 29, 1913.

Buzz, Buzz !

is just the kind of miscalculation Miss Darragh can be perfectly relied upon never to make. Her acting is an affair of the nicest calculation ; to employ a military term, she attains her objective, and we are not to impute a fault if the objective is limited. She keeps her imagination under control ; will you, the spectator, be good enough to keep yours under control also ? It is her place to lead and yours to follow, though there is none of that going hand-in-hand which characterises the fusing of the limitless actor and his audience into one sentient whole. You, too, are limited creatures sitting at a play, and will be shown just so much as the actress thinks good for you.

You come away from a performance of Miss Darragh saying, "How well that is done ! Yes, that was just the right amount of emphasis ! Wonderfully well calculated, that ! Bravo !" and you applaud an immensely clever actress and compare her with other immensely clever actresses. It has hardly occurred to you that you have been prevented from seeing the character by the very effectiveness of the portrayal. It is in this way that Repertory acting gets its revenge. The Repertory actress sometimes succeeds in sending you away from the theatre *concerned for the character she has been representing* in spite of the inadequacy of the representation.

For, as Mr. Walkley quotes from Matthew Arnold, who took it from Sainte-Beuve, every *genre* has its *écueil particulier.* The rock on which the

" professional " actor is most likely to split is that of showing off his technique for its own sake. Technique in acting, as in all the arts, is a means to an end and not an end in itself. The whole aim and object of the actor's technique is that he should breathe life into the actor. The actor who *lives* on the stage is a great actor ; the actor who gives an *imitation* of life, however marvellous the *vraisemblance*, is not. This gift of living in front of an audience is not to be analysed and is hardly to be acquired by taking thought. Tragedians have lacked it, clowns have possessed it abundantly. Coquelin, stout and middle-aged, could play you Cyrano in the morning and M. Jourdain in the evening, putting on their several existences like a suit of clothes. He *was* Cyrano and he *was* the *Bourgeois Gentilhomme*. Sir Herbert Tree would have put on the clothes and composed his features, and the result would have been two wonderful pieces of character-acting. Dan Leno is said to have possessed in superabundance this trick of living on the stage ; to me Mr. Albert Chevalier and Mr. George Formby are more " alive " than Mr. H. B. Irving or Sir George Alexander, neither of which clever and capable actors is ever successful in preventing you from seeing through the cleverness to the actor beneath. I have attributed this failure to come to life to the possession of too elaborate a technique. The alternative, that is, lack of sufficient technique (the art which conceals, etc.), is altogether too damning.

Buzz, Buzz !

It is interesting to compare the acting of Miss Darragh with that of Miss Janet Achurch in two great parts, Shakespeare's Cleopatra and Mr. Shaw's Candida. Miss Achurch, who was, I verily believe, in many ways one of the finest actresses of the modern English stage, had little or no technique. She possessed, in its place, a magnificent power of expression which she seemed to explore afresh at every performance. She would bring off the most astonishing vocal experiments. Her acting had a certain quality of massiveness ; it was not lightly to be turned from its purpose ; there was no beauty of detail, no interest in detail even. She was careless of gesture and clumsy of body, and she played both Candida and Cleopatra as she would have played Brünnhilde. Miss Darragh filled both parts to the brim with the nicest and cleverest calculation. But her effects were not cumulative, and the world was not made empty by the death of her Cleopatra as it was by that of Miss Achurch's bigger-boned Egyptian. Nor could Miss Darragh ever compass the other actress's " That's a good bid, Eugene ! " which resounds in my ears like a stone dropping into a well.

But I set out to praise Miss Darragh. In an English translation of Sudermann's *Johannisfeuer* she was altogether admirable. She had savagery, tenderness, and a kind of gipsy canaillerie. Each act was marked by some extraordinary *tour de force*. There was the long immobility at the table, the shrinking against the door in the terrible scene

148

with the mother, and the nervous surrender to her
lover with the taut clasping of the chair and the
white, drawn face peering at you over the back.
In this piece she had all the intensity and authen-
ticity of emotion that are in danger of shrivelling
up a play so that you find yourself taking a kind
of surreptitious joy in mere technical splendours.
A vicious circle. . . . In the same writer's *Das
Glück im Winckel* Miss Darragh succeeded in
getting and keeping the whip-hand of her many
clevernesses and in achieving a little miracle of
melancholy and regret. Her acting in this play
had the quality of autumn leaves. In lighter
comedy of the order of *The Tyranny of Tears* and the
Walls of Jericho she could sparkle with such brilliance
that the authors of the plays can hardly have known
them.

The Irish Players

" HE passes away under a cloud, inscrutable at heart . . . unforgiven, and excessively romantic. Not in the wildest days of his boyish visions could he have seen the alluring shape of such an extra-ordinary success." This closing sentence from Mr. Conrad's indictment of the romantically minded might well serve as epilogue to Synge's tragedy. The novel may be called a justification *à rebours* rather than an indictment, and Synge could call *The Playboy of the Western World* a comedy. For these playboys of Synge's and Mr. Conrad's are of a world in which plain things cease to have plain meanings, death transfiguring to new and strange kinds of life, and failure leaping to amazing success. " There's a great gap between a gallous story and a dirty deed," says Pegeen, and it is the right-thinking citizen and not the artist who will be keen to echo her. It is a pity that the savagery of the burning of Playboy's leg is softened on the stage, out of deference, one must suppose, to the feelings of people who might see in it only an un-pleasant physical cruelty and fail to recognise the conscientious persecution, the petty inquisitions of the *bourgeois*. Pegeen, as she burns his leg, has a " God help him so," much too beautiful to be thrown away. And this artist, this playboy, fails to win Pegeen—fails, lured on to success beyond the understanding of the plain people of the play, the vision of unending romance. He is the triumphant lover of the whole actual world. The

boast of the Playboy, his vaunted murder, is actually
accomplished by the despicable widow Quin. Only
Christy makes a wonderful song about it, so that
there ceases to be a murder, the glory of the song
blinding us. The widow Quin destroys her man
in the commonplace circumstances of *actual* murder,
ignominious, trite. We imagine that Synge attributed a real murder to one of the characters, and
conveyed it in a contemptuous half-dozen lines to
show his indifference and the indifference of his
Playboy to the actuality of their themes. This
soaring away from facts is the very essence of the
play. Even the Playboy's love-making is not
love, but love of the words love uses. Christy in
his last scene with Pegeen is more self-conscious
than Romeo. He tortures himself to fresh images
of beauty :

Let you wait to hear me talking, till we're astray in
Erris, when Good Friday's by, drinking a sup from a well,
and making mighty kisses with our wetted mouths, or gaming
in a gap of sunshine, with yourself stretched back unto your
necklace, in the flowers of the earth.

And then spurred on by Pegeen's awe and hush to :

If the mitred bishops seen you that time, they'd be the like
of the holy prophets, I'm thinking, to be straining the bars
of Paradise to lay eyes on the Lady Helen of Troy and she
abroad, pacing back and forward, with a nosegay in her
golden shawl.

The whole beauty of the scene lies in the Playboy's real indifference to Pegeen except as a theme

151

for love, and in the interweaving of glamours, his
for his words, hers for him. It is not simple
malice on the widow Quin's part that she calls
Pegeen " a girl you'd see itching and scratching,
and she with a stale stink of poteen on her from
selling in the shop." Nor is it an irresistible
Zolaesque impulse of Synge's, the uncontrolled
passion of people other than artists for seeing things
as they really are. The point is that Pegeen, or
another, will do for this lover. The Playboy goes
away, defeated and glorious in the end, heedless of
her.

It is almost a pity that the part is played by
Miss Maire O'Neill. One would like to see Pegeen
as a wild, ignorant, healthily good-looking girl,
dans le vrai, exactly as she may be supposed to be
" in real life." Miss O'Neill has glamour, radiance,
and all the wonder of Christy's Helen of Troy and
the holy Brigid speaking to the infant saints.
Christy's glamour loses force when it becomes
rational and sincere. And once get sincerity into
this little play and you turn it into a perverse and
curious horror. Bring it in contact with truth and
its miracles of shunning fade and its fine evasions
are away. It is a marvel of artificiality like its
author's style. The Playboy bestrides a dung-
heap. In his prose Synge twisted and compelled
the country speech to his liking, shaping its common
beauties into rare and precious things. The Irish
peasants talk Irish-English, certainly, but not the
Irish-English of Synge. Let us rid ourselves of

stories about listening, note-book in hand, through chinks in floors and walls. That is a necessity of letters that writers should hide. Synge's writing is so little Irish that Irish people have been known to ask the meanings of sentences. It is, rather, an extraordinary mosaic made up of very beautiful Irish things, but no more " natural " than the most careful and precious inlay.

And when it's dead he is, they'd put him in a narrow grave, with cheap sacking wrapping him round, and pour down quick-lime on his head, the way you'd see a woman pouring any frish-frash from a cup,

is the speech of a nervous, sensitive modern. " Cheap sacking," the definite horror of it, betrays the man of letters as sharply as does the cricket-cap in the ballad of the man who was to be hanged. Synge is definitely an artist, dealing in the humbug that the art of writing must always appear to be— to plain people. " He goes away from a living woman to celebrate his pitiless wedding with a shadowy ideal of conduct." So the Playboy, and so too every writer. And this play is the singu-larly perfect work of a singularly perfect writer, who renounced real life for shadowy ideals and ideas of living, and gave up real language for the realities of a more perfect beauty. It is conceivable, even probable, that Synge cared little about his peasants. It is certain that he cared passionately for his writing about them.

Synge's *The Well of the Saints* was beautiful to

Buzz, Buzz !

read, and proves extraordinarily stimulating on the stage. In this little play Synge shows the power, common to all great creative work, of transfiguring his material, of seeing things and making us see things as though they were newly created. The words used last night are possible peasant utterance, but we are not to suppose that the author took a victoria to see the peasants, as one French realist said of another, or that the play is a verbatim transcript of the jottings of a note-book. The talk of these poor folk comes to us through the artist, that saving wall between us and a so-called realism. The theme is brutal enough for any realist—the healing by a saint of a pair of blind beggars, the man's revulsion at the revealed ugliness of his wife, his desire for the first beautiful woman he sees, her contempt and rejection of him, the old couple's miserable compromise. Zola would have given you every cut of their soiled feet, every horror of their rags, every dark place in their souls. Synge walks the road in fellowship with them. His is creative work, and the angels of heaven, the pigsty, the common muck of the road, the passions of men and women are all assimilated with equal zest and given back to us with the old relative value as between each other, but of new and equal loveliness in his exquisite and self-conscious prose. Take this description of a dirty day :

When I was roused up and found I was the like of the little children do be listening to the stories of an old woman, and do be dreaming after in the dark night that it's in grand

The Irish Players

houses of gold they are, with speckled horses to ride, and do be waking again in a short while, and they destroyed, with the cold and the thatch dripping, maybe, and the starved ass braying in the yard.

Every word in this passage leads you unfalteringly to that amazing last line, the " starved ass braying in the yard," at which the picture flashes complete. Or again :

A little drop of water is enough to make the blind see as clear as the grey hawks do be high up, on a still day, sailing the sky.

It is the artist, not the peasant, taking you through these successive degrees of intensity of expression :

Whitish yellowy hair does be soon turning the like of a handful of thin grass you'd see rotting, where the wet lies, at the north of a sty.

This startles one as though the words had been newly made to fit the thing expressed. It is English as elaborately found, for all its artlessness, as Flaubert's French.

And Synge does for his people what he has done for their speech. The theme is no longer ignoble, squalid, mean. When Martin Doul, inarticulate poet in real life, articulate only when he speaks through Synge, leaves the church healed, and makes his way to the beautiful Molly Byrne, shrinking instinctively from the hag in whom he does not recognise his wife, the audience laughed a little—audiences always laugh a little—although the thing is pitiful. His belief in the continued loveliness

155

Buzz, Buzz !

of his wife has been the blind old man's comfort. The lie always comfortably maintained · by the village is exposed, and Martin is torn between loathing of his wife and desire of the beautiful woman. Zola would have shown the animal ; Synge shows the poison of disillusion, the inveterate poet in the man going out to the first loveliness he has known, and, perhaps strongest of all, the horror of old age and the imminence of decay. " It's a few sees the old women rotting for the grave." It would be a mistake to imagine that the play is all high tragedy or even tearful. There is extraordinary comic bite to much of it and a deal of honest laughter. Merciful darkness falls upon the old couple again, and they realise, he that he will have a glorious white beard, she that she will have soft white hair the way there won't be the like of her in the seven counties of the east. " Sight's a queer thing for upsetting a man," they decide, declining the offer of a second healing. They are inveterate romantics. " The idea of " their hair contents them. What would they do with their sight, " the way we'll see our grey hairs falling each day and turning dirty in the rain " ? They are content with their unknown kingdom, the kingdom of the blind ; the humming of bees, sweet smells, and the warm night, the sense of flying things racing in the air, the gentle wind, and the sunshine. Synge's blind folk pray for these as seeing people pray for daily bread.

What writer, now that Synge is gone, could

The Irish Players

do better than Lady Gregory the fecklessness that masquerades as high adventure, the high-falutin that takes on a robe of poetry, the wordy riot, blather, and spate tumbling and tossing to Romance ? In *The Image* of Lady Gregory, these common stone-cutters, carriers, farmers, seaweed-hawkers suffer a sea-change. Pottering bodily within circumscribed limits, they do actually and royally range the stars. They are idealists riding recklessly for a fall. And an idealist, too, without consciousness of his idealism, without artistry, without any sense of play. Brian Hosty's ideal or image was the flowery province of Connacht, seen by him with passion, by the others for the honest naked waste it is. The stone-mason, Coppinger, dreamed of a monument he should raise to a great man. The old midwife transfigures a " blemished little maneen having a stuttering tongue," once her husband, into a " fair-haired boy of Heaven." Malachi Naughton, the mountainy man, makes himself an image of a man greater than O'Connell or Parnell, a man compounded of all sublimities. The play is simple. It starts with a storm, the finding of a mystically lettered board, the stranding of two whales. The profits of the whale-oil are to be devoted to the general good, since none can trust his neighbour, and a statue is to be erected since it cannot advantage one more than another. And since Connacht and Munster cannot agree in the matter of a hero, Hugh O'Lorrha, the mystic name on the wreckage, is chosen. The business-like

157

Buzz, Buzz !

English promptly approve, send down plans from Dublin and a member of Parliament to officiate. Disillusion follows hard. Coppinger's image is destroyed when he finds that he is incapable of building a statue ; Malachi's ecstatic image crumbles at the contact of the ideal and the real. These idealists come their pitiful croppers through simpleness and sincerity. There is nothing of the playboy in them to keep their ideals sky-high immune from working tumbles ; they cannot keep up the pretence of hitching their clumsy waggons to the stars. The moral, drawn by old Peggy Mahon, is that image-makers earn their own defeat when they throw down the images of others, that dreamers must hide their secrets in their hearts. Lady Gregory draws a finer moral, that the dreamer must declare his dream though its betrayal shatter his own perfect vision. " We must say ' God love you ' to the image-makers, for do we not live by the shining of those scattered fragments of their dream ? "

If the matter be all Lady Gregory's, some of the manner is Synge's. In Peggy Mahon we get the very accent of *The Well of the Saints* : " Why would any person go set their mind upon the hither side of the grave, and not upon the far side ? I have seen them come and seen them go, the scores and the hundreds, the same as if they came on a visit to a neighbour's house, and went from it again the time their clothes would be wore out and tattered. And the skin to be wore into rags, the soul is the one thing always "—here Lady

The Irish Players

Gregory speaks with her own voice—" for it was the breath of God put into Adam, and it is the possession of God ever since. I know well where my own mind is living yet, and where I will come to Him when the Lord will send for me."

This recognition of the voice of Synge, now heard through Lady Gregory's, now booming distantly, is no part of complaint. Lady Gregory has her own accent, a little more shrewd perhaps. Witness the certainty of the messenger from the English that the guardians would care nothing for a statue erected to abstract virtue. " Who the hell cares about liberty ? It is what the Board made sure you had the name chosen of some good man." Or the grievance of the stone-cutter confronted with the difficulty of the Dublin designs. " It's a queer thing, now, not to get a picture laid down by some skilled person would be used to going through stone, and to be leaving it to the fancies of young pups of boys rising up." In their grander moments these master-builders are over-articulate, topple headlong from mighty verbal peaks. The English have been confounded for never knowing when they are beaten ; the Irish never know when romance has beaten them. In Lady Gregory it is intrinsic honesty, simplicity, and directness that break her peasants ; one touch of make-believe and they could have climbed again.

The play acts, as we have half-regretfully to admit that these Irish tragi-comedies do act, like rich farce. Perhaps this is inevitable ; Falstaff on

Buzz, Buzz !

the stage is primarily a fat man. So, too, this hairless, toothless humanity of Lady Gregory's, scattering grotesque challenges of valour, can scarcely hope to prate of harps in the air. The wonderful thing is that they do. These divergent thrusts and pulls are at once baulking and stimulating, eye and ear sending the brain contradictory messages for deciphering. Mr. Sinclair shone throughout with comic splendour, and yet a tone in his voice, or the fall of a sentence, would send you straight to Villon and the hardness of prisons or the needs of the belly. You were allowed to hover above the part and the acting, seeing things that were surely never consciously there. And that is the mark of all great acting, that it seems better than it can have been meant to be. Is Mr. Sinclair, in another play, conscious of extraordinary beauty when he tosses his stick into the lonely bed ? Does Lady Gregory realise the rare value of her deflated ending, calculate the full virtue of her disappearing, incredible whales ? The theatre would be a less marvellous place if we could be sure of finding the answer.

Mr. Weedon Grossmith

WITH the handsome exception of the art of Mr.
Weedon Grossmith, and since the death of that fine
tragi-comedian, James Welch, there is scarcely any
English comic acting, as distinct from clowning,
that one would care to disclose, say, to the French.
The responsibility of comic acting is greater than
the tragic stuff's ; the tragedian stalks through life
uninterruptedly, the comedian's way lies through a
distracting maze of tempting irrelevancies. The
tangle is too much for the English actor, a fine side-
splitter, but no preserver of the humanity of his
buffoons. Who that has seen a good French actor
as the father in *Frou-Frou* can forget the incredible
transition from the comic intriguing of an elderly
fribble to the pathos of an old man's distress ? A
French actor will get himself so entirely into the
skin of the part that the pathos will be imminent
from the beginning and the early comedy not
forgotten at the end. Each half will enrich the
other, and we do not get, as on the one occasion
when we saw the part done by an English actor,
two splendid playings of two irreconcilable characters. It is not claimed for Mr. Grossmith that
he has the explicit gift of pathos, but rather that
his comedy, with its Pett - Ridgian insight and
sympathy, is become the pathetic, or as good. The
face is wonderful. The actor has not sponged all
expression from it, as Coquelin did, remodelling the
clay at every new character. Mr. Grossmith has
not got the " bunch of countenances," but he has

Buzz, Buzz !

evolved, superbly, a mask, a permanent actor's mask, to fit the trivialities, smallnesses, self-sufficiencies of his Tidmarshes and Preedys. The nasal sniff, the shrug of the shoulders, the hands outspread in deprecation, the thin lips, the bland forehead, the sleek, submissive hair, with its foolish parting, all go to make up an encyclopædia of insignificance. It was said of an old actor that he played the gentleman with a slight infusion of the footman. So, too, Mr. Grossmith ; but in return he will endow the flunkey with a cast of gentleness. It is difficult to decide exactly how much of this acting is venom, how much a plea in mitigation ; the portraits are so utterly malicious. And yet one feels that the actor has an inkling of his victims' basis of lamentableness, their best of intentions. *Mr. Preedy and the Countess* is the least amusing play of Mr. Carton's that I remember ; or perhaps I should say it is Mr. Carton's play in its least amusing form. The usual racing metaphors have given place to bridge slang, and the managing great lady of whom the author is so fond is this time allowed to be in the scrape herself instead of being on hand to pull somebody else out. Mr. Grossmith has not too much scope as the gentlemanly little provision merchant. Yet he has talk of " sleeping apartments," and of a ham that is " less abundant " than he thinks. And he wears throughout the evening his wonderfully deprecatory smile of bewildered yet steadfast innocence, of underbred yet imperturbable gallantry, of unmerited misfortune light-heartedly bearing up.

162

Pélissier

THE height, weight, and girth, the habit of the player and the tricks of his body are as much the property of the public and the concern of criticism as the configuration of temperament and intelligence. Irving recognised this when he bent and subdued his genius, twisted brain and mind to accordance with a personality which, as the " humble servant " of the public, he knew it was his business to lay at their feet. Actually he did very little twisting and torturing of his own mentality. It was the mentality of other people that had to do the submitting—the Sardous and the Shakespeares ; it was the actor's rôles, the absurd Robespierres and Dantes, and even the Hamlets and the Lears, that had to accommodate themselves. There are many definitions of acting, and all of them include the exploitation of the personality of the actor. Old Irving knew perfectly well the salient features of his personality. The simple and popular impression of him, and the first answer a foreigner would get to his question as to what our great actor was like, was to the effect that his legs were preposterous and that you could not hear what he said. There is no doubt that Irving did his best to accentuate the popular impression, that he maintained a studied oddity of gait — he could walk about a room naturally enough — and that he wilfully elaborated an individual and eccentric code of articulation.

Now one supposes that the first impression of

Buzz, Buzz !

Pélissier was one of an exceeding fatness, an impression carefully fostered by a comedian alive to the values of the flesh. The critics did not waste time in euphemisms as to " amplitude " or circumlocutions about " fulness of habit." Appreciation of Pélissier's quality as an actor began, as it did with Irving, in a distinct and explicit recognition of a grotesque personality on which the comedian had as much right to insist as the tragedian, and perhaps even more need. And here one comes upon a curious contradiction. If the actor's personality is to be considered an integral part of his art—and we remember that it was so in the tragedian's case and in the cases of the late George Weir and Henry Kemble, whole merchant's ventures of the comic spirit, both of them, and mountains of pure flesh—how was it that Pélissier's more unctuous revellings in portliness were amongst the least of his successes, that his studies in the colossal could be quite unamusing, that he so often contrived to shear adiposity of its natural quaintness ? The explanation was to be found, one thinks, in the curious divergence in this actor between his intellectual temper and his " exteriors." Weir and Kemble were all for the *œillades* of the audience. They relished the "appetite of our eyes." They would echo Falstaff's " Sometimes the beam of her view gilded my foot, sometimes my portly belly " in a perfect *crescendo* of justifiable pride. Their temper was a simple affair of generosity, somnolence, rumination. Pélissier's

164

spirit was quite other; it was critical, judicious, and faintly acid. He would have resented Pistol's " Then did the sun on dunghill shine " and Nym's zestful applause. Pélissier could not write a ditty about the amours of a toothbrush and a sponge without conveying a whole criticism of sentimental ballad-singing and the people who indulge in it. The study of " Réjanehardt " was a merciless exposition of the technique of French acting, a scathing exposure of the ridiculous basis the sublimities have, on occasion, to put up with. His " Voice Trial " was a surgical joy, and if ridicule could kill, the lighter stage must long ago have bled to death. It was only when the actor descended to frank fooling that he got the most out of his personality and the least out of his wit. The Comic Spirit must have laughed up her sleeve when she fitted so steely a soul to so generous a body. In a word, if the actor was not always elementally funny, he was always an indictment. In simulating a series of preposterous deals between an enraged amateur and a broker in " objets d'art et de vertu," he would give a complete representation in buffoonery of the whole commercial life of a city. In burlesques like *The Whip*, gorgeous in fidelity to Drury Lane, Pélissier's clowning rose to great heights. He had a Gargantuan inebriety of bewilderment, a dæmonic power of innocence smacking of black magic. Sometimes he would stand in the middle of the stage, utterly unable to compass another word, a mass of quaking stolidity, not, like

Buzz, Buzz !

the old actor in Lamb, primarily astonished by the elemental sun, moon, and stars about him, but the tongue-tied victim of his own improvisation and exuberance.

Miss Vesta Tilley

Miss Vesta Tilley's almost delirious welcome and the crowd's delighted taking up of the burden of each song—as who should say the audience at the Paris Opera House and the March from *Aïda*—the roar with which familiar symphonies are greeted, should be a sufficient warning against any show of superciliousness. Here is something which a large public wants absolutely and goes on wanting. Miss Tilley sang four songs, the newish " That's the Time a Fellow wants his Ma," and the old " Seaside Smile," " Jolly Good Luck to the Girl who weds a Soldier," and the " Idol of the Girls." Not a very well-bred programme in cold print, a trifle vulgar perhaps, a bit " com," as Mr. Welch's ever-delightful Mr. Hopkinson would keep on explaining to the Duchess.

But we have little to do with questions of breeding in these creations of sheer delight. When the curtain goes up for Miss Tilley there is borne upon the house the familiar feeling of proficiency, of old mastery and finish. We know beforehand that the big stage will be filled more completely by the tiny figure than by any other in the music-hall world. Miss Tilley's consciousness of her power to hold us is matched by the proud acceptance of her welcome and the immensity of her desire to please. Her trim little shape is alive with gratification, radiant of inconceivable atomies of good-will. Every day that she plays is turned into a fête-day, dull Mondays become Saturdays, and Saturdays

Buzz, Buzz !

Bank holidays. One has little sympathy with those hypercritical persons who object that this actress's range is limited. Our main concern is that her art is quintessential, that within the tiny range of the schoolboy out for a lark, the swaggering recruit, the pier-head " clurk," you get all that is vital and all in them that matters. These little people are as well done as Henley's London Types and as admirably differentiated. Or you might say that they have the pluck of good photographic negatives. Dandyism is given its full value. Miss Tilley will out-Brummell Brummell, and she is insistent that her modes shall be masculine—a Burlington Arcade masculinity, if you will. Some purpose of symbolism underlies the gorgeous parade. The unbuttoning of a coat serves to let you into the secrets of a second verse and the hidden mysteries of a character not more than waistcoat deep, whilst the cock-sure tap settling the hat is to stand for the assertion that these young men are " all right." Of course they are all right ; they make up the backbone of the country ; they have grit in spite of their knocking down of bobbies and tasting of every kind of " wet " or whatever the present-day game and its present-day idiom may be. These " Champagne Charlies," as another generation used to call them, are, Miss Tilley is never tired of showing us in penitential and contrite last verses, the " right stuff." But these little codicils of seriousness are not to be too insistently urged. One prefers the portrayal of youth in its first headi-

Miss Vesta Tilley

ness, the immense zest, the interpretation of life
akin to the spirit of the street-boy in Elgar's *Cockaigne*.
" Et in Arcadia ego," or its equivalent, muse our
Percys and Sydneys as, packed in their eighteen-
penny stalls, office and paper cuffs left behind, they
listen critically to some ditty of the seaside. And
indeed the songs have a smack, not of the sea, but
of the band and the crowd at the pier-head.

Fred Emney

ALL the world is the poorer for the loss of Fred
Emney. It was at Arles in the south of France that
I heard of his death, and I needed no help from
the indistinguishable smudges in the halfpenny
journals to recall the broad countenance of fun,
the roving, bibulous eye, the high-pitched yet
masculine voice, the rolling gait which would lurch
rather than steer to the chair and table, composing
with bed and box the entire *mobilier* of this astonishing " Mrs. May." I can see him now in the
habiliments of the monthly nurse as she lived—for
live she did upon the stage in absolute verisimilitude.
I can see the door in the exact mathematical centre
of the garret's infamous back wall. I can see it
opening to disclose the equivocal figure monstrously
bedecked, grotesquely turban'd, the neck swathed
in a " boa " of fabulous cockatoo. I see again the
elastic-sided boots covering traditional bunions,
the chamois leather gloves protective against the
devastating effects of the grate's black-lead. I
hear the dissimulatory cough of the dissembling
midwife as she fumbles for the intonations of gen-
tility. " Is Mrs. May h'in, my good woman ? "
The preamble is a trifle uncertain—mere nerves,
however. With the success of the plot the voice
steadies to the superciliousness proper to Mayfair.
Again in recollection do I hear the colloguing at
the door, the mind's eye and ear gladdening afresh
at the dignified entry, the infinite affability of this
visitor of distinction.

Fred Emney

The imbroglio is adequately preposterous-history, as the French say, of a monthly nurse in debt to her landlady. " Pay up, or you go ! " is the harped announcement of that virago. The midwife receives a call to an urgent case in the country. " Pay up, or you don't go ! " is now the tune. And so Mrs. May—the very name is redolent of brass plates in back streets, significant only to the worldly-wise—Mrs. May has recourse to stratagem and to the finery of an actress on the next floor. In monumental disguise she assumes the personality of a wholly fictitious sister, whose air of affluence is to renew the credit of her temporarily embarrassed relative. With what glee do we follow the unequal combat, the visitor gaining in the grand manner as she loses in strict sobriety, the landlady going under to her sense of snobbishness, her common 'cuteness an easy victim to her sense of social distinction. She attempts a faded rivalry ; she would have it understood that she, too, knows what horses are : " My pa kept *a quantity* of 'em, but nothing would induce me to go near 'em—— " She agrees that gin is " common stuff," professing to have it in the house " in case of measles." But it is essential for the reader's comprehension that he should have a taste of this absurd dialogue, and I append a slice of it as nearly as my memory serves me. The reader must imagine the exaggerated drawl of Emney's " Mrs. Le Browning " and the common patness of the lodging-house keeper :

Buzz, Buzz !

Mrs. Le Browning. Is Mrs. May h'in, my good woman ?

Landlady (doubtful). Well, no, Mum, she ain't, Mum. Won't you sit down ?

Mrs. Le B. Strange, not h'in ! Didn't she get my telegram ?

Landlady. She 'ad a telegram, Mum ; I brought it up with my own 'ands.

Mrs. Le B. Well, I won't come h'in.—Will you please to tell 'er that 'er sister, Mrs. Le Browning, 'as called ?

Landlady (impressed). 'Er sister ! Oh ! I might 'ave known it, Mum, from the strong family likeness. Do come an' sit down, Mum. Mrs. May won't be long.

Mrs. Le B. Well, I'll come in for a few minutes, but I daresn't wait longer, or the 'orses might get cold.

Landlady. Why not try a motor, Mum ? I've an 'orror of 'orses. My pa kept a quantity of 'em, but nothing would induce me to go near 'em.

Mrs. Le B. (with indifference). Oh h'indeed. The h'only thing I object to in 'em, they make such a fearful dust. Do you know, my mouth is full of it ?

Landlady. Could I presume to offer you a cup of tea, Mum ?

Mrs. Le B. (politely). There's nothing I should like better, but I daresn't. You know, tea h'acts like poison on my system. It does, I assure you.

Landlady. I can quite believe it, Mum, you being accustomed to the best of everything. But is there nothink I could offer you ? Your dear sister'd be dreadful worrited if she knew you was dry and wouldn't take nothink.

Mrs. Le B. Well, if you should 'appen to have a little *barley-water* ready, Madam.

Landlady. There now, I 'ad some in the 'ouse only a month or two back. If you could wait for an hour or two. . . .

Mrs. Le B. I wouldn't trouble you for the world (*with*

172

Fred Emney

social ease). I suppose you 'aven't a little drop of Madeira
sherry wine ?

Landlady. No.

Mrs. Le B. No, then, don't worrit. You know the
doctors order me gin, but it's such common stuff I suppose
you don't keep it in the 'ouse ?

Landlady. Well, Mum, to tell you the honest truth, I
have a little. What I keeps in the 'ouse in case of measles.
If you'll excuse me for a minute. . . .

Mrs. Le B. Oh, serpintly, serpintly.

Landlady. If I'd known I was going to 'ave the pleasure
of seeing you, I'd have 'ad the h'other. I shan't be a minute.
(*Exit Landlady*.)

Mrs. Le B. (*in a crescendo of violence*). Ah, you wicked
old cat, you ! You wicked old. . . . Done 'er ! done
'er ! (*Subsiding*.) She don't know me ! She don't know
me ! You know my aunt, my Aunt Ermyntrude was
right. I'd have made a fortune on the stage. (*Mimicking*.)
I shan't be a minute. (*Voice rising to a scream*.) Bah !
you old faggot, you ! you wicked 'ussy ! you BRAZEN
'ussy, you ! (*Subsiding again*.) I knew she kep' it. And
when I asked 'er to lend me 'arf a quartern or so only the
other day she swore she never 'ad none. But she ain't
reconised me yet. Now I'll lead 'er on. (*Enter Landlady*.)

Landlady. Your dear sister said to me only this morning
—Daisy, dear, she said, if my sister was to call 'ere, she says,
you'd know 'er by my likeness to me, she says—Well, love,
I says, all I can say is, she must be a very good-looking lidy.
Any water, Mum ?

Mrs. Le B. (*in the actor's own deep voice*). No water,
thank you.

Surely this absurd dialogue, compact of the
low-conditioned humours which are the common
property of the music-hall, is as true to Dickens as

Buzz, Buzz !

Dickens was true to life.   Now there is a point at which all art in its portrayal of humanity must fall short of actual flesh and blood, though any such statement is the flattest critical heresy.   In sheer despair will Dickens describe and redescribe the attributes of Micawber, the walk, the air, the genteel roll in the voice, always using the same words over and over again in an attempt to force them to a higher degree of expressiveness by sheer reiteration. Lamb finds himself in similar plight when he would reduce an actor to the printed page.   In conscious effort to force words to a higher power he will expend on a description of a work-a-day actor the Pactolean treasures of inexhaustible imagery. And that is why you find him investing the acting of Munden with talk of Cassiopeia's chair, Platonic ideas, constellatory magnifications.   He would make us wonder as he himself wondered, at the fertility, the richness, the variety of the actor.   He would, one thinks, have used similar means to make us wonder at poor Emney's great creation.   Expressiveness was in every inflection of Mrs. May's voice, every cock of the actor's eye, every readjustment of the tumbling spectacles, in the veerings to the floor, in the way he would come to anchor by the chair.   The scissor-like propulsion from door to table had all the nice calculation of the drunkard ; the denunciations of the mean-spirited landlady were so many delirious trumpetings.   " Brazen hussy " could have come only from a throat of brass. And then there were the shrugs and leers and

Fred Emney

winks, a complete outfit and armoury of hints, of euphemisms, of wrappings-up, of calling things by polite misnomers. In Mrs. May the whole of the ritual of the profession stood revealed. Here, you felt, was a riotous old hag, whose mind was a jumble of " interesting conditions," of " being worse before being better," of grotesque sympathies and jocose encouragements. She trailed baby-linen ; she was implicit with the mystery of cauls. The illustrations to Dickens contain one picture which may give some faint idea of the physical presentment of Mrs. May—the drawing by Phiz, " Mr. F.'s Aunt is conducted into Retirement." In both countenances we find the same stony implacability, the same riotous bewilderment, the " yonderly " expressed of a stern and much-tried nature *aux prises* with Destiny.

Yes, the world is indeed the poorer for this actor's passing. One would bestow on him an old-style farewell. May his voyage to the Shades be less ignobly harassed than his earthly travellings ! Deal leniently with him, Pluto ! Charon, thou " murky rogue," as Lamb called thee, be not too insistent on payment of thy fare ! " Pay up, or you don't go ! " was the earthly menace. A like threat, O Ferryman, and thou doom'st thy fare, stripped of whatever securities a tin box may afford, to wander everlastingly on the hither shore. At the coming of the Egyptian lovers Dido and her Aneas were to want troops. It is in my mind that by now Egyptian banterings may have grown stale and

Buzz, Buzz !

that the house waits for our homely comedian.   Is
it too daring a speculation that, with bonnet awry,
the familiar figure is now fumbling at the latch ?
" Your door *does* open, doesn't it ? "   Is it unlawful
to suppose that the lips framed to old habit are
waking the ghostly haunt with their familiar and
pertinacious " Is Mrs. May h'in ? "

III
Mr. Cleever goes to the Theatre: A Parable wherein is determined the Temperament of an Artist

A UNE CHANTEUSE

Un fifre qui piaule et siffle d'un ton sec,
Un basson qui nasille, un vieux qui s'époumonne
A cracher ses chicots dans le cou d'un trombonne,
Un violon qui tinte ainsi qu'un vieux rebec.

Un flageolet poussif dont on suce le bec,
Un piston grincheux, la grosse caisse qui tonne,
Tel est, avec un chef pansu comme une tonne,
Scrofuleux, laid enfin à tenir en échec

La femme la plus apte aux amoureuses lices,
L'orchestre du théâtre—Et c'est là cependant
Que toi, mon seul amour, toi, mes seules délices,

Tu brames tous les soirs d'infâmes ritournelles,
Et que, la bouche en cœur, l'œil clos, le bras pendant,
Tu souris aux voyous, ô la Reine des belles !

J. K. HUYSMANS.

TO A MUSIC-HALL SINGER

Bassoon of the stopp'd nose and crazy flute,
Trombone which toothless age and worn-out lung
Blow until breath be spent, thereafter mute,
The whining fiddle and the whimpering tongue
Of rusty cornet, wheezing, whistling fife,
Loud blatant drum and, perched upon his stool,
The bellied leader, all his body rife
With foul disease and ugliness to cool
The woman aptest for the game of love :
Such are the players—Yet on this poor stage
You with hoarse ditty infinitely move
Me to the memory of old love and rage,
Whilst with red mouth and lax luxurious mien
You tease pale cut-throats, O my Beauty's Queen.

Rough translation.

I. Heredity

The Child is Father of the Man.
WORDSWORTH.

EDWARD CLEEVER, critic of the provincial theatre, which is by no means the same thing as a provincial man of letters, first saw the light, as tiresome novelists have it, one bright September morning in the late 'seventies. A Londoner by instinct, he had the topographical misfortune to be born into a family housed in red brick on the extreme inner edge of the Lancashire moors. The scene of our hero's birth was the quasi-rural, quasi-manufacturing district of Hoddendale, the *milieu* tallow-chandling, the *décor* one of those homely mansions so deftly and pathetically described by Stanley Houghton in one of his accesses of Pierre Loti-ism. But the reader would do wrong were he to jump to the conclusion that Cleever's father bore any resemblance to the Nathaniel Jeffcote of Mr. Herbert Lomas [1] or his mother to the Mrs. Jeffcote of Miss Daisy England.[1] There was, in point of fact, nothing of *Hindle Wakes* about the good couple, of whom it is significant that their dual insistence on attendance on alternate Thursdays at the classical concerts of the then Mr. Charles Hallé was as heart-whole as the single determination of the bread-winner never to be found missing from his post of duty on the Tallow-chandler's Exchange. Truth to tell, my hero's bent and genius were of that whimsical nature which is too often the despairing outcome—let

---

[1] Members of Miss Horniman's Company and original creators of the parts in *Hindle Wakes*.

179

Buzz, Buzz !

Mendel explain it as he will—of a line of decent forbears and of immediate parentage of transcendent merit.

It will not be unavailing if we begin our inquiry into the mind of erratic and unstable genius by soundings as to heredity and environment, both of which alarming terms will be shown to mean that our hero was very much what his parents had made him and not he himself. When old Mr. Cleever set out from London to make his fortune, he turned, as was the custom with the Dick Whittingtons of a generation ago, his face Northwards towards the large tallow-chandling centre of which Hoddendale is but a pleasant annex. There he had the good fortune to fall in with a north-country lady with whom times had gone so hardly as to justify the letting of " professional apartments." Young Cleever, as old Mr. Cleever was then, was mothered by a landlady who insisted on Dickens, Thackeray, and Sir Walter, lent her countenance to the stage-representation of certain of the plays of Shakespeare, and whiled away her lodger's winter evenings by performing on the piano with him *à quatre mains*, thereby counteracting the attractiveness of the too theatrical ladies who throned and queened it in her front rooms from Sunday night to ensuing Sunday morning.

In these front rooms Snevellicci succeeded Petowker in procession of tawdry similarity, curlpapers and wrappers the wear for afternoons, evenings a blaze, if not of glory, then of a very praiseworthy tinsel.   On occasion an actor of repute or singer from the Italian Opera, provided credentials were good, visitors standing in greater need of recommendation than the rooms.   On these respectable and masculine occasions young Cleever— we are still speaking of Cleever *père*—was encouraged in the minor civilities, the helping on of overcoats, the fetching of slippers, the drawing of refractory supper-corks, as warmly as in the frailer instances he was dissuaded from too great an attentiveness.   The good lady held, not in wild unreason, that you may admire an art and look askance at the artist.   She would frown on the too cordial appreciation of a *diseuse* whilst holding it proper that the more asthmatic members of an Italian chorus should have an arm offered them in the winter's fog, and the elderly actress fallen on worsening days be attended to and from the stage door.

This influence for good was rarely seconded by young Cleever's employer, a man of kindly nature with the proselytising knack of imposing on his young men his own particular brand of religious opinion, a plain one and a straightforward.   Our young man drew to maturity with a mind well stocked with a sensible dogma, a sound commercial morality, a knowledge of good books and good music, and the traditional inkling that all that glitters on the stage is not necessarily gold in the lodgings.

Gold of the purest was to be found in the land-

Buzz, Buzz !

lady's daughter, who once a year came glinting home from Paris, whither her mother had despatched her, to the impoverishing of her already straitened means. But the heroic lady, fearing nothing of a " come-down " save the change from gentle condition to the genteel and the coarsening rather than the widening of acquaintance, chose to suffer privation and divorce from an only daughter that the child might not suffer the common contacts which are the sting of poverty. The little girl, who was of course to become Mrs. Cleever—old Mrs. Cleever as will soon appear—added to her inheritance of gentle condition the best of educations and an intimate knowledge of the manners, tongue, and mind of the most gracious people in the world. Were this a full-length novel I would tell of the transplanting of this fine flower of French culture to her proper soil, of her orphaning, of her battle for a living, of the standing in good stead of the French language and a perfect mastery of the piano. I would tell how her mother's protégé and staunch champion transferred his loyalty to the child, how he waited for her, worked and prospered for her, rose to partnership for her, built for her honour and comfort the red brick house with the considerable air to which finally he took her as his bride. An ordinary sequence of events at which there is little to marvel unless it be the perfect loyalty, constancy, and devotion of these otherwise unremarkable people. But as my tale is not to be a long one, and as the discovery of the romantic in the humdrum is not new, we will pass, if you please, to that later period when the union had been blessed with three children, of whom the youngest, Edward, is to be our hero.

II. Environment

Train up a child in the way he should go . . .
Proverbs.

HEAVEN, we are told, lies about us in our infancy, choosing for its vicegerents the children's mothers. In these modern times all mothers are fairy godmothers, inexpertness in the art being inexcusable since first Miss Hilda Trevelyan played Wendy. I am, I confess, at a loss for the word which shall give the atmosphere of protective idolatry which has pervaded the nurseries of the world since children first were. Some word there must be alike for the Madonnas of Raphael and the reverential hat-lifting low-comedian. Every mother knows the word—so Mr. Barrie is never tired of telling us—and I am urgent for my readers to understand that Mrs. Cleever had as fine a sense of it as any Mrs. Darling. But it were better I do not persist in this quest of a word lest I hang up my tale till the reader's patience is exhausted. Sufficient that Mrs. Cleever crooned it to Edward as she had crooned it to Stephen and John, bethinking herself the while that if actual bestowal of virtues be the prerogative of immaterial godmothers, it is the privilege of mothers in the flesh to hold up before the eyes of their little ones those attributes which they most desire the child to choose for himself.

Now it is not to be supposed that Mrs. Cleever made conscious parade of the beauties of life. She was just her own beautiful self. It just happened, then, that the walls of the nursery were hung with portraits of *maestri* in place of the usual sand-boys,

184

donkeys, spades, and buckets, that the child's eyes closed on Handel in a periwig and opened on Mendelssohn in a choker. One picture it took young Cleever twenty years to figure out—a portrait of a Mr. Thorne with his head on one side apparently in the act of anointing himself with a purse. "As Figaro" was the disturbing legend. Nor was it with intent that the boy was nightly hushed with strains from *Norma* and *La Sonnambula*,[1] floating up through door and staircase. Never in after life could Cleever hear without a massing of the clouds of infancy the fateful opening of the "Fantaisie Impromptu" of Chopin. Thoughts which were in existence before the immensely later period of words would haunt him his later life through at the first notes of the "D flat Waltz" of Chopin—the one with the click of horses' hoofs in it. Schubert's "Impromptu in B flat" would inflict more sadness on his childish soul than it was strong enough to bear, the Fourth Variation wetting his pillow miserably. The "Invitation" of Weber would give him an outrageous feeling which he was afterwards to know as Romance, whilst the "Rondo in E flat" made him unreasonably happy. The impatient hurryings and scurryings in what he was also to know as "rubato" passages, the reluctant slowings-down called later and to infinitely less purpose "rallentandos," were so many promises of mysterious and ineffable glamour never to be fulfilled in the grown-up world. In less fanciful phrase

[1] Leybach's and Thalberg's arrangements.

185

Buzz, Buzz !

they were part of the familiar spirits and friendly presences of the night nursery, having for allies the gleam of the night-light and the flicker of the fire in the child's nightly battles against the shadows on the wall and the fearful creak of the stairs. If you had told him that the strains of *Casta Diva* which generally soothed him to sleep were part of the music of the spheres, he would have nodded with as competent an understanding as any full-blown opera-goer of us all.

Sometimes his Mummy, as he called her, would bend over his cot and kiss him good-night a little earlier than usual, smelling extra sweet and looking particularly beautiful, with gleaming arms and " empty " throat. He would ask where she was going. " To the theatre, Mischief," she would reply, putting off further questioning with a " You'll know when you are a big boy ! "

Then came the time when the child was allowed to sit up to see his Mummy set off in state for the place with the funny name. On these occasions there were sweet-scented gloves to finger, a fan to wonder at, and glasses to peer through which made things either too big or too small, whilst his father, wearing a low shirt, would munch a biscuit and sip some strong-smelling stuff out of a decanter. Then he, Stephen, and John would be packed off to bed to play at theatres by opening their nighties and baring their chests, till Nurse would get very cross and mutter something about catching deaths of cold. Then in the morning the two older boys would be

got out of bed at seven to do their hour's practice
before they went to school, the faint whine of the
fiddle at odds with the thud of Kruger's exercises.
It would seem that the music of the spheres is not
the same thing in the morning that it is at night.
The devotion of Mummy and Father, who every
morning permitted this infraction upon their sleep,
did not occur to the boy.

At other times his parents would go off to a
place they called " The Concert," but this was
obviously a much soberer affair, a matter of bonnet
and dolman for his mother, who was met by father
" at the Club."   So that although " The Concert "
was doubtless a very nice place, it was clearly to
be ranked amongst the smaller joys, since there was
no dressing up for it, and no French gentleman to
come in to do Mummy's hair, pat the boy on the
cheek, say he was growing quite a fine lad, and
that he would take a glass of claret, thank-you.

The theatre passed through many phases of
misconception in young Edward's mind.   In the
big book-case in the library there were a lot of
volumes called *The Illustrated Penny Magazine* with
1840 and similar numbers on the backs.   It was to
these that the boy would turn for elucidation of
the many mysteries of which the world seemed to
be made up.   In these wonderful books in which
the tower of Pisa seemed to bow gracefully across
the pages to the young Queen of England in her
diadem, hock-bottled shoulders and coronation
robes, there were pictures of tournaments and jousts

187

Buzz, Buzz !

and all the different kinds of armour worn by knights and their horses in Tudor and Plantagenet days. As these pictures were the most wonderful things as yet presented to the boy's consciousness, and as " The Theatre " was the place his mother liked best, he came to the conclusion that this last must be the place in which knights in armour broke lances, whatever that meant, for fun. He often questioned his mother about the horses, and she would answer, " That's a circus, Mischief." This idea of what a theatre should really be like persisted even after the boy had been taken to one of those highly coloured places of amusement.

Besides the *Penny Magazine*, the library contained some wonderful books called " Shakespeare," the pages of which were enlivened with attractive pictures of knights in armour—obviously the same knights as in the Magazine—leaning upon their swords, whilst a vassal held their horses and a herald blew a trumpet and called a parley with other knights on the top of high battlements. It was a handsome edition, beautifully printed on paper that gleamed like ivory and crackled when you turned the pages. For many years Shakespeare was associated with Sunday evenings when, after the hymns, his mother would take down a volume for him—the one with the picture of the hunchbacked Gloster for preference—which he would turn over whilst she read aloud a story of a little boy called David who bit his stepfather's thumb.

In the summer the boy's brain would lie fallow,

its owner being fully occupied with being a horse
which his two brothers drove in turns. It was
towards the end of his ninth year that he realised
what sort of places " The Theatre " and " The
Concert " were, and why the former was so much
more splendid than the latter. At a concert you
sat at a dizzy height, about eight feet actually, above
the platform and watched a great number of people
help to play a band. At intervals a stout gentleman [1]
with white gloves and shiny, carefully arranged hair
would sing and bow a great many times, and a lady [2]
who apparently could not get on or off the platform
without the assistance of a kind-looking old gentleman [3] with a sad, grave face and cheeks like pouches,
would play on a piano of quite a different shape
from his mother's. But a theatre was a place which
made your heart beat so fast that sometimes you
could hardly bear it. There you sat quite near the
performers, all of whom had eyes as big as saucers.
The play had been *Robinson Crusoe*, and even the
newspapers thought it a wonderful play, since every
day they told you on the front page that it was a
" gorgeous pantomime " and an " enormous success," printing each statement twelve times over.
Besides, you were taken to a concert in a tram and
an ordinary railway carriage, whereas to a theatre
you went in a cab and a much more beautiful
carriage. And a concert was not so very exciting,
but after a theatre you could not sleep because your
eyes burnt so that it hurt you to shut them.

[1] Mr. Edward Lloyd.   [2] Miss Fanny Davies.   [3] Sir Charles Hallé.

Buzz, Buzz !

A year or two slips by and young Edward
begins to take a more reasoning interest. He
notices that when actors from London are come
to the neighbouring town there is a stir in the house,
and that his mother makes great pretence of teasing
his father into a box for the play, whilst his father
makes equal show of being overborne. Well does
he know that his good lady is as capable of independent action as that Casterbridge Jenny who
stole from her husband's side for a last dance at the
Phœnix. But the theatre is in the blood of both
and little pressure is needed. On one immensely
eventful Saturday evening the boy is taken to see
Hamlet, goodness knows who in the sables. What
fire is in the boy's ears all the way home and during
the droning of next morning's preacher, to whose
sermon old Mr. Cleever enjoins his sons' particular
attention, doubtless as counter-irritant to the dangerous stimulant of the previous evening. Already it
is in the recognised order of things that the theatre
is a pleasure for which atonement has to be made.
The boy is not yet of an age to understand that
both father and mother are merely trying to drive
the Artistic Temperament double with a Sense of
Duty, and that they are taking Religion or at
least Church-going on to the box to steady the
coach. *But the mischief of presenting the theatre
as a forbidden delight is already done.*

It is at dessert after the middle - day Sunday
dinner, the cloth removed, and the decanters gone
round that the theatre resumes sway in the old

190

gentleman's blood. Wife, children, and whatever guests there may be, listen in silence to his stirring criticisms born of a life-long adoration of the theatre. Doubtful though it be whether plays have ever existed for old Mr. Cleever save as a vehicle for acting, certain it is that never have actors had such discerning tribute since the days of Roscius. Certain judgments were repeated with such solemn assurance, fervour, and frequency that they became part of the critical fabric of young Edward's mind. Never, to the very end of his career, could Cleever doubt that Salvini's Othello had been the greatest piece of tragic acting of any era, although run fairly close by the Hamlet of Edwin Booth. This dictum must be taken as typical of a score of others with which I will not weary the reader. Then came the time when the boy was given opportunity for some appraisements of his own, being treated in quick succession to Henry Irving as an ill-used English king and a very terrible French one, an innocent gentleman barely escaping execution through resemblance to a highwayman, a murderer choked in his sleep by an imaginary rope, a pathetic Jew and an old clergyman, whose daughter ran away and so grieved the old man that he fell to mumbling his sermon in his sleep. Each performance in turn seemed to the boy to be the most tremendous experience of his life, but his father was not to be shaken from the dictum that the actor was " mannered." Then came the great day when, after a long debate, he was allowed to accompany his parents

Buzz, Buzz !

to a performance by a great French actress. He
gathered that if he had been a year or two older
the play would have been forbidden, but his mother
had urged that it would be a pity to deprive the
boy of a great recollection. All of which puzzled
him very much. Of the performance he understood
little, save that the French lady seemed to have the
power of making people tremendously happy and
then tremendously unhappy. He remembered
afterwards that when the lady in the play died his
mother cried a great deal, that everybody in the
house cried a great deal, and that he himself cried
in sympathy. He remembered, too, his father
insisting in a very shaky voice that the French
actress was " not a patch " upon another French
actress who had died long before, which seemed
very ungracious. But then his father was always
like that and could always tell you how much better
acting had been when he was a boy.

When Edward attained to an age when he could
cross swords, first with his older brothers and then
with his father, Sunday's dinner-table became a
battlefield. The children would all be under the
spell of Irving, whereas the old gentleman, although
admitting that on the previous evening the actor
had been stupendous, terrifying, and not entirely
to be contained within the laws of nature, would
insist with querulous vigour that he could not
cross a stage decently nor declaim a line. The
case of Ellen Terry was considered tragic, though
you could hardly let it go at that. This actress,

said the father, had been the wittiest of Portias, the loveliest of Violas, exquisite as Imogen, heart-rending as Cordelia, as Beatrice a sunbeam. He had never seen nor would any ever see the like of her April gift of tears and laughter, her apple-blossom sense of Shakespearean comedy. And yet this darling bud and magical flower of English acting—here the old gentleman would grow lyrical—could be seen throwing herself away on clowning Nance Oldfields and preposterous French washer-women. And once when Edward asked timidly whether any more beautiful woman had ever existed, old Mr. Cleever would lay it down that, strictly speaking, the actress had not a single classical feature in her face, but that not to resemble her was not to be beautiful at all.

The tendency of the sons, as they grew up, to urge an intellectual aspect to the art of acting would throw the old gentleman on to the strict defensive and a flat insistence on the purely emotional, an attitude in which he was strongly seconded by his old friend Manuelo, the famous Spanish tenor and descendant of a line of tenors. The grizzled singer with the head of a lion, the touzled mane and burnt-out eyes had, some thirty years previously, been a fellow-lodger with Mr. Cleever at the pro-fessional apartments. The two friends were in passionate agreement as to the superiority of the old school of Bel Canto over the new-fangled tyranny of noise ; they differed not a hair's-breadth in their estimates of Bellini and Donizetti, Rossini

o

Buzz, Buzz !

and Meyerbeer. The old artist would illustrate the musical intelligence of the great singers of the past in terms of endless cadenzas concocted at the singer's will whilst operas waited, conductors laid down their batons, and audiences drank greedily the ceaseless flow of meaningless impromptu. Nor were there material differences in the old friends' judgments of the singers of a bygone age, —Rubini, Persiani, Tamburini, Lablache, Grisi, Mario, Christine Nilsson, Jenny Lind. The children would listen in awe as these great names, thick with the dust of the past, were bandied about, shaken and aired into some kind of momentary freshness. Agreed, too, that Bernhardt could not efface old memories of Rachel, that Macready had always been too much a gentleman to be a really great actor, that the world had seen the last of its Phelps and its Fechters, its Charles Mathews and its Alfred Wigans. With one voice they would declare intellect to have no place in the art of acting, citing a notorious writer of intellectual plays who had refused to impart the meaning of a rôle to an old-fashioned actor on the ground that he played it magnificently by sheer force of temperament and in perfect innocence of intention. Together they would declare the stage the lair of iniquity and corruption, the player a temperamental rascal fit only to be kept in compounds with his familiars and released during the hours of performance.

In a word, the theme of the French writer's " Ceux qui ont beaucoup de sensibilité ont toujours

mauvais caractère " all over again. The old singer
with entirely Southern frankness would enlighten
this singular dinner - table with first-hand reports
as to observed discrepancy between artistic achievement and moral impetus. He would tell of a
famous basso topping the scroll of fame whose name
was a byword in the sinks of Europe ; of an actor
at whose pathos the public would drop tears faster
than the Arabian trees their medicinable gum,
making a lame defence against forgery and petty
theft ; of a wife dragged at the heels of a thousand
scandals betaking a bruised body and hurt mind
to the theatre, there to weep at the spectacle of her
husband's admirably - mimed adorations. " Brutes
in ecstasy," thought young Cleever, framing his
first criticism. The old man would recall the scenic
storm-tossings of souls infinitely mean, the heaven-
kissing ecstasies of lips framed in intimacy to un-
truth. He would quote Balzac—for the old singer
had some reading—as to the cathedral tenor thrilling
the fretted roof and reflecting, " Have I perhaps
eaten too much macaroni ? " Talk such as this
would prolong itself till dark, when, on rare occasion,
the old master would sing an air of Grétry or Lully,
the " O Paradiso " of Meyerbeer, or that exquisite
little song of Gounod, " Au Printemps."

About this time young Edward discovered,
tucked away in an old bookcase in the housekeeper's
room, a precious and altogether improbable collection of books. Improbable if you do not realise
that old Mr. Cleever had never been afraid of book-

Buzz, Buzz !

shops even in his jaunts to Paris. There, safe from disturbance, lying on his stomach, equally at home, thanks to his mother's teaching, in French or English, young Cleever would pore over Maurice Alhoy's *Les Bagnes, Histoire, Types, Mœurs, Mystères* ; translations of Anacréon and Sapho ; Cerfberr and Christophe's *Répertoire de la Comédie Humaine.* (Long before the boy had read a line of the novels he was a fervent Balzacian.) It was a strange collection. *Les Diaboliques* of Barbey d'Aurevilly and the comedies of Marivaux, Beaumarchais, and Crébillon ; the *Proverbes* of Alfred de Musset, *Vathek, La Nouvelle Héloïse,* and the *Mémoires* of Casanova. He read indiscriminately, dipping now into *Tom Jones,* now into *The Confessions of an Opium-Eater,* enchanted indifferently by Harriet Martineau and Shelley, Jane Austen and Théophile Gautier. There were incredible books too, such as *Les Sérails de Paris, ou Vies et Portraits des Dames Paris, Gourdan, Montigni et autres Appareilleuses. Ouvrages contenant la déscription de leurs Sérails, leurs Intrigues, et les Aventures des plus fameuses Courtisanes.* Three books he always read by stealth, fearful lest the door should open on his reading. They were Foxe's *Book of Protestant Martyrs, Les Facecieuses Nuicts du Seigneur Straparole,* and *Le Putanisme d'Amsterdam, livre contenant les tours et les ruses dont se servent les putains et les maquereaux, comme aussi leur manière de vivre, leur croyances erronées, etc.*

It is not to be imagined that during all this time

196

the boy was allowed to neglect the more ordinary
enlightenments. He headed each of his forms in
turn, joining in the games with indifferent execution
and perfect apprehension of their spirit. His
masters were an impetuous young classicist who
was bored by Caesar and pitchforked his startled
pupils into Horace, a Foreign Language master
who could discover humanity in *Bérénice* and
elegance in *Wallenstein*, and an imperfectly appreci-
ated author who devoted his evenings to the com-
position of decadent masterpieces and perfectly
understood young Cleever's distaste for gymnasium,
swimming - bath, carpentry, and bug - hunting.
Cleever's scholastic career came to an end in the
usual blaze of glory when at the end - of - term
Speech Day he carried off the Shakespeare prize,
delivered himself of the " Rondo Capriccioso " of
Mendelssohn without a mistake and as much feeling
as that sentimental and characteristic piece deserves,
and declaimed as a last firework the speech from
Le Cid beginning " O rage, ô désespoir, ô vieil-
lesse ennemie." It is worth recording that after
this latter performance he avowed to his father that
as an actor he feared he was not much good. Whereupon the old gentleman gave his son a pat on the
back in recognition of the youngster's critical
perceptiveness.

" I agree with you, my boy. Not worth a
damn ! And never will be ! " he said cordially.

III. Sowing the Seed

. . . and when he is old he will not depart from it.
Proverbs.

CEPENDANT, as the French say when they want an excuse for a fresh paragraph, it was not until these talkative Sundays came to an end—which they did when old Mr. Cleever died—that the young man had any idea of their extraordinary influence over him. During his father's lifetime it had seemed natural that the predominant interest of a family should be the temperament of this actor, the technics of that. The years between his father's last talk and the son's first article were coloured by recollection of the old gentleman's passion. Never could the boy forget the lighting-up of feature, the animation of voice and gesture, the smack and relish with which the older man would touch to life the theatre's old bones. Once when he had ventured on some expression of astonishment that his father had never written a book about the theatre, had not been impelled to crystallise his recollections—

" ' Impelled!' burst out his father, ' Crystallise!' Remember this, my son, that when you have a business to make you will be impelled, as you call it, to crystallise on that. My old employer would never engage a clerk who played the fiddle! He was afraid of a competing interest! As for professional dramatic critics, they are scoundrels to a man, tuft-hunters, hangers-on, and worse. Yours is a different pair of shoes my boy. You're a young gentleman at large, or will be, and if you think you've anything to say about acting—not but what

198

Sowing the Seed

you're a damned poor judge from all I've seen of
your enthusiasm—you are at liberty to fire away.
Only whatever you do, be honest ! If you think
some poor fool of a Juliet wants tying to a cart tail
and whipping, don't spare her. It'll hurt her more
than it'll hurt you." And the old gentleman would
fall to telling of how Oliver Wendell Holmes—who
should have known better—went round late at
night to the office of a famous London newspaper
to try to mitigate a critic's anticipated rigours as to
the Juliet of Madame Modjeska.

For Cleever criticism had many blandishments.
There was the discoverer's interest, the " Come and
see what I've found ! " of a boy happening on a bird's
nest. There was the keenness to place and define,
to deflate and to see justice done. There was the
passion to right old wrongs, to resettle old quarrels,
to affirm and reaffirm Malibran's superiority over
Pasta, to start old thrills at the mention of Barry
Sullivan, to arbitrate among present-day supremacies.
Add the sentimental craving for the rescue and
perpetuation of the transcient glory of the actor.
The tender passage,

> Et, pour que le néant ne touche point à lui,
> C'est assez d'un enfant sur sa mère endormi,

had suggested, the day when first he came across
Musset, the reflection that if the painter stood in
little need of the poet, the actor stood in very urgent
need of adoration handed down by fathers and
perpetuated by sons. " So utterly blown are the
paper roses of their fame," is a line from Cleever's

Buzz, Buzz !

first essay " On Some of the Not So Very Old Actors." Last item in this catalogue of motives was the sense of what is due to the critic's own self-consciousness. What matter that this self-consciousness was to concern itself with the virtuosity of vagabond players ? There is a kind of inverted sublimity in concentration upon inessentials. The dinner-table had taught Cleever that acting is three parts of life., Given a grief, a dilemma, or a disaster in terms of his own existence and Cleever promised himself to revel in the *scène à faire*.

Cependant, you do not become a dramatic critic merely by wishing to become one. Provincial newspapers lay out their criticism in a way which is both haphazard and cast-iron. The untidy young gentleman who bowdlerises the proceedings at the Council Meetings will finish his day's work with a notice of the later Quartets of Beethoven. The rakish young gentleman and dead-spit of Henry Irving in the 'forties will flit from a fat-stock show to a dissertation on the Rokeby "Venus." The writer-up of sensational murders will sound the stops of the new Hamlet. But these young gentlemen are clever enough to fence themselves in with an iron ring. They are shy of the amateur. It was in competition with them that Cleever had first to elbow his way, for with all his *idea* of the theatre, he felt himself to lack the journalist's 'cute and common proficiencies. He felt that as yet he was not weight enough for The Paper, that august institution over which the great Lake so awfully presided.

Sowing the Seed

It is rare that a man fails to win a thing if he will it hard enough. And Cleever had to will hard to persist in his long siege to publicity. What lunches to chief reporters, what dinners to sub-editors, what truckling to thin wits, what subservience to these *littérateurs* of the middling manners ! Cleever wrote and submitted trial notices, ironical, raffish, gay, trivial, sincere. They were not, editors regretted, what their readers wanted. . . . At last, after much insuccess, Cleever got his chance. A parson with the mania for reconciling *coulisse* and vestry had trumpeted in the halfpenny Press a reading of the lessons by the foremost light of the hole-and-corner, unlicensed, Sunday-afternoon Drama. Cleever had retorted with a colossal *blague* on the theme, " Should Divorced Actors go round with the Plate ? " taken seriously by some common fellow of an editor, who used it to build up a vulgar and profitable discussion. Nothing for it, too, but that the young spark who could create such a fuss should be given a trial. With a single bound, then, at one fell swoop of questionable taste, Cleever got his chance.

" On to a paper of sorts, now to justify myself ! " was at this period our hero's version of Rastignac's *A nous deux maintenant !* At once he found himself up against several propositions, as our unlettered friends have it. The first, the old predilection of the public to have its back scratched. " Never try to elevate your public," wrote the great Lake in an encouraging letter. " Twenty years of laborious attempts in that direction have taught me to regard

Buzz, Buzz !

the public as a more than usually wilful pig, and dramatic criticism as the ring through its nose. The amount of grunting and squealing you get is out of all proportion to the progress achieved. And if you are not very strong in the wrist, the fool-pig goes backwards."

Second proposition, the crass conceit of a public holding that no lack of study or training in an art is any bar to the plain man's right to a plain opinion. Fifty years ago Hector Berlioz could write, " C'est convenu, chacun a le droit de parler et d'écrire sur la musique ; c'est un art banal et *fait pour tout le monde* ; la phrase est consacrée ! " Since Berlioz' day we have extended this prerogative of free criticism to the theatre. Everybody has the right to his or her opinion, no more value attaching to trained criticism than to the amateur and uninformed. " If I was at the play I know whether I liked it or not. If I wasn't what does it matter ? " babbled into his ear at dinner by a pretty woman would incline Cleever to contemplate the massacre of a whole sex.

Third proposition, that whereas the public is keen to insist upon criticism refraining, like charity, from vaunting itself, the very essence and gist of criticism is that it shall be egotistical, uncompromising, and authoritatively puffed-up. A whole year was spent by Cleever in butting his head against this triple wall of stupidity.

To *épater* the bourgeois is, as has often been shown, a parasitical thing, dependent on the inverted approbation of inferiors. To *épater* the Great Man of your art, to hasten the moment when, in the early Italian manner, he shall take off his hat and say, " Pupil, you are the master. Our rôles are reversed ! "—this is legitimate ambition. With this aim in view did Cleever follow in the footsteps of the great Lake ; finding them at the start many sizes too big for him. After a time Cleever became conscious that the difference between his powers and Lake's was lessening. The visit to the town of an actor of note would be the occasion for a match of wit between the two critics. At first Lake was invariably the winner, but soon Cleever would find himself snatching an odd success. He felt, for instance, that he had scored with " passionate insincerity" devised for our best tailored and genteelest mannered carpet-knight. Then, when an undersized and essentially Metropolitan little gentleman came down to present a servile footman *aux prises* with a dukedom going a-begging, and Lake had put himself out to add to English literature another Lamb's essay on the valets of Jack Bannister, Cleever had come in nicely under the great man's arm with the prick that the heroes of this comedian were by genesis and derivation so many " standers behind chairs." Or the younger man would come up to the net and bring off a smash by declaring that Sir Johnston Forbes-Robertson was Meredith's " Phoebus Apollo turned fasting friar " all over again. At last the day arrived when Cleever, had he been a painter, would have summoned Lake to

Buzz, Buzz !

his studio, and Lake, before the masterpiece, would have bared his head or removed his shoon.   As it was, Cleever could only hope that Lake would spot his " notice " in the columns of The Paper's half-penny rival.   The play had been one of the duller " Henry's," the actor a romantic, Roman-nosed visionary, the Don Quixote of the stage.   As the player elbowed his way through the text with the breathlessness of new discovery, now ranting, now quiescent, now lashed to perfect recollection of his lines, now making good the blanks with the froth of Elizabethan jargon blown about the surface of this actor's temperament—as Cleever watched the gaunt, ungainly figure ranging the scene, trailing the verse with as insolent an impunity as the *banderillero* his cape, there came into his mind the line,

Bulls that walk the pastures in kingly-flashing coats.

And Cleever knew that the days of his critical apprenticeship were over.   " A nous deux maintenant ! " he could say to himself in earnest, shaking a hopeful fist at the office of The Paper.   And the following week Lake capitulated.

" You had better come over to us," he said.

So ended our hero's first year of criticism, a year of tireless preparation, of not treading upon earth, of defeats at the hands of the Idea, of victories over mere words.   Of minor satisfactions too.   You may picture him sitting at supper in a gayish restaurant, his night's work done and only awaiting a last tinkering and retouching according to the inspiration of his cigar ; the crowd of comedians, tragic when they are not raffish, supping at the neighbouring tables and heedless of the amused irony with which Cleever would daintily steep his pen as he smoked. A year of belated strolls in the deserted streets—his notice handed in at the newspaper office—to the wan paling of the gas lamps. A year of wondering how his stuff would read in the morning. A year, finally, of unswerving admiration and dazzled worship of Lake. A year in which Lake shone undimmed.

IV. Crime

It is the cause, it is the cause, my soul.
Othello.

(Ten Years Later)

" Now," Edward Cleever found himself saying, " or
never." The alternative, the possible " never,"
boomed in his ears with the insistence of a mouthing
actor. " Never " did not seem to be worth making
so much fuss about when the " now " might be so
deftly and easily applied, and the highly uncritical
state of affairs brought to an end and mended with
the end of the man to whose " Life and Criticism "
he was ready to put the finishing touches. If
Cleever held his hand, then Lake would still go on
being alive and refraining from kicking, however
definitely Cleever's clever study of him might label
the old vigour and kicking-power as the real Lake,
and the forbearances, withdrawals, qualifications,
and compunctions as the simple decadence of a
Great Man. The apprehension, the significance
of the " now " made Cleever throw down his pen.
He was tired of the purely physical tedium of
writing, tired of his notice, tired of all " earnest "
acting, tired of the intellectual young men who
could knock the bottom out of the profundities of
a Galsworthy, only to be hopelessly floored by the
amenities of a Maugham. They managed to get
distinction, did these young men, into the khaki
and broad arrows of the convict. Why, in the devil's
name, when they attempted dress-clothes, did they
ape the manners of the invoice-clerk and affect the
206

accent of the common young gentleman in Mr. Stanley Houghton's *Hindle Wakes* ? At this agreeable point in Cleever's meditations there came to him from the next room and through the half-open door Lake's genial and cheery " Let the beggars have it, Cleever, let the beggars have it ! " And Cleever knew that the older man had arrived at that point in his notice when the most infamous of sticks was being gently " perhaps'd " into adequacy with the note of credit due to him as a trier. Lake's cheerful encouragement, always a welcome interruption, was not needed to bring Cleever to a sense of his surroundings. He was acutely aware of The Paper in all his, for him, high-minded moods. Its generosity had sometimes come near to hurting him. Robert Lake, the biggest gun of them all, had not stopped short of rescuing him from the halfpenny rag of his first start, at putting him on his feet, but had steadied him when he got on to them. The recollection in the immediate now of Lake's simple kindnesses was not welcome ; Cleever had quite enough to do to put the big obligations behind him. He supposed he could not deny that the thing he contemplated might by normal people be called dastardly. It was difficult to steer clear of normal ways of thinking. Even in the event of its being called not only dastardly but treacherous, he had behind him, he reckoned, ten years of schooling and steeling in treachery, treachery to himself that is, in the daily task of keeping within the bounds of The Paper's com-

Buzz, Buzz !

punctions. That night's play, for instance, had been acted with incredible banality even for the Stokes Theatre. But the Stokes Theatre was a laudable institution, and from him as critic was expected elaborations of wariness and the most tactful of sheerings-off.

This matter of squeamishness, of going mercifully when the impulse was all for slashing, had been the last thing to be learnt in Cleever's long apprenticeship, and almost as big a stumbling-block in a professional career as his vanity, the vanity of the enraged amateur. To understand Cleever, to get full measure of the littleness of the man, a littleness scarcely atoned for in any recognised moral scale by his extraordinary *flair* for acting, you must know something about this vanity. Cleever divided his readers into three classes, and he never omitted to make his little study in classification in the tramcar which every morning took him down to his business in tallow and kindred commodities. The bad readers didn't read him and that disposed of them. The indifferent read on indifferently without resentment at interruption. He knew the indifferent lot, the way they fumbled for coppers, lifting their heads like disturbed sheep, and dropping them to the paper again only to browse on a fresh patch. He knew to a blade where they had left off, and the feeling of being baulked by them, of being robbed of the chance of getting something into their dull heads before the business of the day dulled them

208

still further, would stick to him for the rest of the
twenty-four hours. Stranded in the middle of his
delicate adjustments, they would babble over some
counter of the way The Paper had come out strong
that morning, not giving that fine thing of his a
chance, not even giving themselves the chance, sheep
that they were, of tumbling to his clever little trick
of deflation, his pet last sentence or two's sticking
of the pin into the bag of preliminary fulsomeness.
They would insist on making a full critical meal of
his *apéritif*. Worse still, that silly indignation of
theirs when he had taken all sorts of nobility for
granted and was finding fastidious fault, not with
some recognised halo, but with the fact that on a
particular evening it had been worn a little awry.
The perfect reader—and he was always cock-
sure of him—looked for his initials at the foot of
the column, fascinating proof of his power to stagger.
If you are ever to get to know Cleever intimately,
you must know that he would just as soon stagger
little folks as great. He had never lost the stagger-
ing sense, he had mastered so completely the
theatre's impudent charlatanism, relished and absorbed so fully its magnificent chicanery, that
charlatanism and chicanery had become his very
soul. But his *flair* for the theatre was only strength-
ened, and as long as that fine sense of his and the
power to stagger people remained, he was quite
careless of deterioration in that other, the intellectual
as opposed to the temperamental side of criticism.
And he was quite genuine in this matter of stagger-

ing people or of being staggered. Let others
dazzle him who could and welcome ; he felt that
he could help them through their hoops. He had
his own particular feeling for duty too. It was
rare that, having written his notice, he failed to
put in an appearance at the theatre at least once
during the evening, not so much to guard against
the dirty trick the theatre might play him of being
inopportunely burnt to the ground, but rather to
reward the general craning of necks towards what
in the provinces passes for a stall, his stall, notoriously his and The Paper's.

Here was Cleever, now, scratching for something
to say of an actress over whose lamentable best
he had spent a desperate evening. He wanted
something of the polite and malicious. It wasn't
quite fair of people to do their pitiful bests, to come
the human being over him. What of the boots
that let in water, the pinch of hunger, the querulous-
ness of unpaid landladies ? He winced delicately
at the idea of these unspeakable things and gave a
sharper turn to the screw of savagery in his notice.
He realised that his humanity was as keen as anybody's, more delicately appreciative, perhaps, from
the fact that it was closer to prying than lending
a hand. How long was it since Lake had lent him
a hand ? It was ten years since his first bungling
yet cleverish article, ten years since he had realised
in a blinding flash that he might do dramatic criticism, that the sheep might come to draw at him
the quick breath of wonder.

Crime

To Cleever's horror, within a fortnight Lake
had hinted at forbearance and encouragement,
putting him up to what he afterwards knew to be
the " note " of The Paper, its dodges of kindliness,
and wrinkles of mitigation. It was borne in upon
him sickeningly that all the good-intentioned people
were to be treated better than their deserts. Od's-
bodikins, but with what infinities of leniency. The
Paper's kindliness seemed to him a perpetual screen
between all well-intentioned people and the short-
comings which it was uncharitable to suppose
them to possess. Between The Paper and human
nature, between The Paper and all knowledge of
life as it is, hung, and must hang for ever, the im-
penetrable clouds of The Paper's own nobility.
Cleever saw himself condemned for ever to this
buttoning of the foils of plain speaking. But,
mind you, the buttons could come off for villainy,
for the scarifying of genuine evil-doers ; it was
for the good-intentioned that a new art, a whole
apparatus of letting-down, was conceived and
perfected.

At his desk Cleever now sat digging viciously
for blandness that should set the town smiling.
Ever so tiny a kink would do, a twist that Lake
himself would not call equivocal. Lake would
have managed to lend his sentence an air of bene-
volence, and here was Cleever stumped for malice !
The involuntariness of the comparison was sure
sign that Cleever was beginning to realise the change
of his attitude towards Lake. He found himself

Buzz, Buzz !

going to church—that was the dreadful thing—
to the moral character of the man to whose art in
his younger days he had gone so religiously to
school. The change, beginning with uneasiness,
had gone on to mistrust with the noting of the
way Lake's scathing wit (for he could be scathing)
had of boiling over in talk and simmering down
to generosity in print.

At this point in his meditation the boy came in
with a last demand for copy, and Cleever, less patient
than usual, let it go unrevised, a mere hotch-potch
of the intelligible. He harked back to Lake.
Strange that the one man of his generation to " see "
the theatre, to revel in the potency of its purely
material glamour, in the frame of it, in the way
the monstrous neck of the double-bass would stand
out blackly against the brilliant arch—strange that
the man who had accepted frankly and greedily
the fard on the white faces of the actors should have
gone so definitely and hopelessly over to the pretended intellectual side of it. " Exits," Lake had
once written, " are ever so much more than mere
endings to scenes, entrances ever so much more
than a condition of their starting. They are themselves of enormous value, part of the wealth of the
theatre, of its trickery, insolent, trivial, superb."
How was it that to the man who once could write
like this the make-up of the actor had sunk to
a convention, a " legitimate " precaution against
physical pallor ? How was it that this great sense
of the theatre was being ousted, as it most obviously

was, by an almost mayoral passion for citizenship ? It must not be imagined that Lake had
lost his craftsmanship, that his decadence was a
thing of obvious nakedness. The old trick of
writing prevailed, but you could feel that the new
intellectual theatre had become the very stuff and
bone of the man in whose blood the old mountebanking had once so magnificently run. You would
not have got Lake to admit that he realised the
connection, or the possibility of connection, between
actors and their standing as, let us say, voters.
You would not have got him to admit that the
effort to use a vote honestly and courageously could
mitigate an artistic enormity, but you felt that the
strollers took rank in Lake's mind, not according
to their playing, but in accordance with their
citizenship. The theatre, one felt, was coming
into line with the Town Hall. " I can conceive
a genius concocting an unhealthy work and the
citizen in him tearing it up," Lake had said ; and
" I can conceive the man of genius annihilating
the citizen," Cleever had retorted.

It is doubtful whether the amateur in Cleever
would ever have decided upon the grotesque achievement of actually putting somebody out of the
way, always a professional matter in its definiteness,
if it had not been for the famous Stokes Repertory
Theatre and the manner in which it was being
coddled by The Paper. This Theatre, conceived,
endowed, and run by one Wembley P. Stokes of
Chicago, a business gentleman of the hide-and-

Buzz, Buzz !

skin persuasion in his own country, of æsthetic
tastes in ours, had none of the unpleasant taint of
the professional theatre about it. No actor was
engaged who had not been an abundant failure in
town; leading ladies were accepted according to
the rigidity of their manners. Playwrights of
admitted success were suspect; the theatre was
given up to comedies of unemployment in the
style of Blue Books and with the imagination of
an election address, or rather two election addresses,
the passionate hearing of both sides of a case now
apparently the be-all and the end-all of the drama.
The stall floor was the apotheosis of the dowdy. And
yet the theatre was losing money ! Wembley P.
Stokes had not succeeded in acquiring the purely
British taste for losing money. He had openly
threatened that if the theatre did not make money
by hook or by crook—and every doleful expedient
had been religiously tried—the theatre would have
to be given up. Lake on The Paper had done his
best. " We simply say that it is no great crime on
the part of these young people that they are not
great actors. It is enormously to their credit that
they make the shots at great acting that they do."
" To err," a later paragraph went on to say, " was
eminently human and actor-like, to forgive, eminently
critical." And so on, and so forth, with the kindly
trail of humanity over it all. Now, Cleever did not
want the Stokes Theatre to go out of existence
altogether. It was worth his while to have a theatre
in the provinces in which people were interested,

if only he could have the opportunity of showing them how magnificently he, Cleever, could take it by the scruff of its neck and shake it into success. But Lake, his senior, stood in the way. Matters were getting desperate. The one actor of talent in the company, inadvertently recruited, had openly talked of chucking it and going back to the " profession." It was obvious to Cleever that Lake was destroying by kindness, had indeed virtually destroyed, the venture. With a hazy recollection of what some German historian has said about it being lucky for Gustavus Adolphus, or some other hero, that he died when he did, Cleever went calmly into Lake's room. He must rid the theatre of this urbane priest.

And now, gentle reader, I warn you that you are about to come upon tragedy. The theatre, with Cleever at the critical head of affairs, made so much money that the management saw no reason why it should not make more. Better acting had been seen with the decline of the advanced play— a decline carefully fostered by Cleever—and even great acting with the production, carefully encouraged by him, of those bad plays in which alone great acting is possible. The Stokes Theatre soon saw no reason why it should not give its public the only really first-rate acting of our time, the acting of the music-hall, where of course the words don't matter. The advertisements in the papers began to run : " No stall-floor in the city can show a braver array of well-dressed folks than the Stokes

Buzz, Buzz !

Pavilion of Varieties. . . ." But Cleever did not succeed in taking to his English music-hall. His essay in despatch, about which normal people would, if they had known, have said quite hard things, was not such a complete success after all. As soon as all the tiresome formalities were over he retired from the whirl and excitement of life in provincial towns, and took up existence in the country, breeding, I think, prize pigs. Such little darlings they were too.

V. Retribution

The fact of a man being a poisoner is nothing against his prose.
There is no essential incongruity between crime and culture. We cannot re-write the whole of history for the purpose of gratifying our moral sense of what should be.

Pen, Pencil, and Poison.

CLEEVER's withdrawal to rural fastnesses was not unattended by a consciousness that his ears might not be entirely stopped against the Theatre's call, or the call of the next best in that line. It was with intense excitement therefore that he paid his sixpence for admission one wet Saturday night into the only theatre the country-side affords, to wit, a travelling menagerie. He found the crowd of bumpkins struck into a very ecstasy of stupidity. They showed no capacity for wonder, nor sense of the extraordinary. With open mouth and lacklustre eye they turned indifferently from Ocelot to Hamadryad, from Clouded Tiger to Pig-tailed Ape. The " entertainment " did not seem to offer more than a choice of humiliations. There was to be lion-taming and a tug-of-war ; Elephant *versus* the village's Picked Men of Muscle. First lions for the humiliating and then men. In the affair of the lion-taming there seemed to be no possibility of deception. There was no doubt but that the lion-tamer's air of bravado and intrepidity was a superb piece of artistry cloaking a physical shivering and quaking. Lorenzo's gait was the gait of a man going to execution ; death was in his loins, eternity in the nape of his neck. Now the crowd drew its breath sharply ; to the women it seemed an urgent

Buzz, Buzz !

matter that the greasy fellow with the " dangerous "
moustache—Cleever was putting their suscepti-
bilities into words—should come through scathless.
What strain of lion-taming would not thenceforward
run through the stock of this innocent village ? . . .
But Cleever realised that the red-hot irons, popularly
supposed factors in the subjugation of recalcitrant
majesty, were not a startling feature of the exhibition.
There were not going to be, in point of fact, any.
There was not going to be for him even a remote
chance of bagging something in the way of sensational finishes, of acquiring a collector's piece of
virtuosity in a lion-tamer's dying. He did not
watch the performance. The elephant was more
amusing. He or she walked away with the thirty
brawny villagers as if they had been men of genius.

" Et puis il se demandait un peu "—Cleever
asked himself what were the sensations genuinely
aroused in him by these Beasts since, condemning
the yokel for lack of emotions, it seemed but just
he should sport some of his own. And it came with
something of a shock to him to have to confess that
he didn't really find emotions, interests even, in the
wearying and banal succession of cages. Now, if
he had been going to write, but stay—he *was* going
to write, that was just it. He would put an article
together for old times' sake. No lack of interest
now, no more drawing of emotional blanks.
Number sixty—" The Griffin Vulture." The decadent was the " line." With what *immondices*
then, had not that beak gloriously dripped ! What

ecstasy of corruption had not been his, second only
to the fury of a Gilles de Rais ! What prosecution
of decay had he not known, this *gourmet* after the
heart of a Des Esseintes. In what unholy crevices
had he not luxuriantly nozzled ; how, like Fan-
freluche, had he not offended in the tousling and
mousling of his victims! Cleever's inspiration dried
up with these playfulnesses. Luckily he caught
sight of a little friend of earlier in the evening,
a monkey who, performance finished, now sat on
an overturned bucket blinking at him with inscrutable eyes, critical yet tolerant of him, he felt sure.
What secrets of the road were not open to that wise
little brain ? He had the " line " again now—the
delights of caravaning, the joy of the road, the
inspanning of curious cattle, the rests by the way-
side, the scent of peat, of acrid smoke blue against
quiet trees, all that intimate mountebanking that
is half Leoncavallo, half Goncourt. Was there not
a passage in a book of his childhood that was
miraculously in the vein ? He wondered if he could
reconstruct it. " Joyce, the cruel father and still
more cruel husband, threw open the door of the
caravan. The sunbeams streamed in through the
little window and, falling on the bed, shone on the
pale and ghastly figure of his wife, now for ever still.
And there, with her arms around her mother's neck
and the wreath of roses fallen from her hair on to
the pillow, lay little Rosalie, fast asleep, with the
tears still wet on her cheeks. She had fallen asleep
on her mother's bed, in her beautiful white dress,

Buzz, Buzz !

just as she had been acting at the play. Joyce swore softly." Cleever was not sure about Joyce swearing softly, but it seemed the probable thing. Then was there not something nicely pathetic to be got out of the death of a boy acrobat in one of Mr. Hitchens' early novels ? Yes—since it seems he must be article-mongering—he had the old ladies of The Paper right enough, and while he was about it, why should he not fetch the N.S.P.C.A. and the members of " Our Dumb Friends' League " ? Some Frenchman had a rattling story, a kind of " Conte Féroce " about travelling shows and the cooping-up of a King of Beasts in a mouse-trap of a cage. The thing was called *To the Christians with the Lions*, and the author had some sourish pleasantries about the present-day Christian's way of getting his own back for the early martyrdoms. For his " advanced " readers, the very young gentlemen who wrote plays about the *amours* of the ward and passion in the operating-theatre, there was always *Une Passion dans le Désert* to quote from. Oh ! but he was forgetting the wind-up of *Manette Salomon*, a magnificent close for him. The hero is at the long last of a spent life in passionate contemplation of a cage of beasts. " His soul became the soul of all the animal creation. Something of him passed into the soul of everything that flies, of everything that grows, of everything that runs. Daybreak, spring, bird-life—all that sings, sang in him. Into his very entrails passed a sheer animal joy, a boundless sense of ruminating felicity

Retribution

in which the Creature attains unity with the Creator."

Cleever remembered how deeply he had been touched—*le cœur crispé d'angoisse*—by the death, in this book, of a pet monkey! What obsequies had there ever been more exquisite than those so gravely conducted by Anatole? " Little monkey gone to Paradise. Little monkey have his fill of cocoa-nuts and eternal sunshine. Little monkey have warm sun on back for evermore! And Anatole took the little beast in his arms, closed his eyes as they were the eyes of a human being, straightened his limbs, folded his tail decently beneath him, and put him in the ground. And with the interment of his little friend Anatole buried for ever his own *gaminerie*." Cleever was not ashamed to admit that this was the passage in all literature that had moved him the most. But then, he was always stirred by something just less than the first-rate. In literature a dead monkey, in the theatre the last throes of sputum-voiding courtesanes, in drawing illustrations in the comic papers of Paris of the deaths of decadent poets. Cleever always heard the second-rate calling to him. . . . He brought himself up sharp. What more would his article want? A touch of the grandiose? *Salammbô* would provide some stately procession of jewelled dromedaries. Of the *macabre*? He could lug in that bit from *The Temptation of St. Antony* in which infamous monsters wallowing in primæval slime unwittingly devour their own feet!

Buzz, Buzz !

And then Cleever had the supreme shock of his existence. In a flash he who had delighted in " seeing " his fellows " saw " himself. It came about in the simplest of ways. He was standing in contemplation of a cage of lion cubs, toying with a phrase. " How infinitely sweet the odour of stripe and spot, how infinitely base the stench of fellow-men ! " How would that do ? Suddenly he heard the voice of a farmer of his acquaintance, a sordid fellow and a grasping. The brute was looking at the cubs and saying to his wife, a thin, stale woman, " Blest if those beggars don't remind me of the bloody kids when they're asleep ! " Here out of this common mouth was quick, living speech ; out of this vulgar mind live, quick emotion driving sweetly and cleanly into the heart of things. " Out of his mouth a red, red rose, out of his heart a white." . . . Here was honesty and sincerity of which Cleever in his heart of hearts knew himself to be for ever incapable. . . . There was—surely this was avowal passionate enough— no heart, no soul, no core to him. . . . He was the charlatan, the humbug, the Artist. . . . He would have to revise his world, he must recognise hence-forth that the simple farmers, the punctual maniacs of morning trains, the common little women who trade in suppers are nearer to an actual heart of things than he. He must recognise that they are in contact with emotion void of cant, even if it be only the emotions of parenthood, of not getting the sack at the office, of getting a line to say in the next

production. He, Cleever, " n'était qu'un artiste."
And there again was the damning thing. Even
when he had at last got hold of a very genuine and
respectable emotion—the emotion of realising that
he couldn't really *feel*—he must needs quote from
some damned Frenchman. Even at the very
instant of making his momentous discovery about
himself he had noted how the woman, *attendrie* at
the mention of her " bloody " kids, had taken her
man's arm. Quite mechanically he had murmured :

> And at some festival we two
> Will wander through the lighted city streets ;
> And in the crowd I'll take his arm and feel
> Him closer for the press.

This was getting pretty hellish. . . .

Cleever became conscious that the show was
closing. Lads were offering their lasses moist palms
for the longest way home. As our hero made his
way through the amorous crowd the crazy band
struck up " The Soldiers' Chorus," and there came
drifting into his mind the words, " The artist
pretends to the ordinary emotions that he may write
about them extraordinarily." He said it over to
himself once or twice slowly. He lingered over the
half-true phrase, caring infinitely little for degrees
of truth, conscious only of infinite comfort, of infinite
healing. He had been extraordinarily ill ; he had
deserted his creed at the bidding of Right-minded-
ness ; he had flung down his banner at the trumpet-
ing of Morality. The artist was, he must insist

223

Buzz, Buzz !

better cattle than these farmers with their legitimate passions and their lawful kids. He would be a Sick Man no longer. " The artist pretends to the ordinary emotions that he may write about them extraordinarily." Never again would he betray his artistry so far as to *feel* a genuine emotion. Pretence is the boundary of the Artist. That much is certain. Never again would Cleever trespass, for on the other side of that fence lies the province of Conduct. And Conduct is a poisonous thing with which your Artist may have nothing to do. For Conduct turns him into a Sick Man and his sickness is the sickness of Death.

VI. Epilogue

The immense artistic advantage of having a company of normal human citizens who do a day's work and go *home* at night, instead of a troupe of wandering mountebanks whose life is the play they are acting.

LEWIS CASSON,
Letter to *The Manchester Guardian.*

The domestic virtues are not the true basis of art, though they may serve as an excellent advertisement for second-rate artists.

OSCAR WILDE,
Intentions.

The ideal mother cannot be the great artist. . . . Hypocrites will write about the Church and Stage, and new devotees will fall before a single shrine of shovel-hattedness and motley. . . . Kensington matrons will incline a more and more docile ear to that which they are now seeking to believe—that their daughters may be virtuous actresses. . . . We shall hear of another queen of the boards who nurses her children, and another who goes to Church every Sunday ; many strange things will come to pass, but such phases of stage-life are ephemeral and circumstantial—gnats on the surface of a well, and in the end the abiding and important truth will be found unchanged at the bottom.

GEORGE MOORE,
Impressions and Opinions.

I love the stage,
And hate to see it made the prostitute
Of crafty godliness. . . .

JOHN DAVIDSON,
The Theatrocrat.

I COME, in this affecting last chapter, not to praise Cleever but to dispose of him. I am to set down as much as I remember of the talk that fell from him when he knew his nights were numbered. Those talks, those eager and swift résumés, ticked off the nights as they slipped all too rapidly away. For the daytime Cleever had never, in current jargon, much use. " The day is all very well for buyers and sellers ; it is at night that one artist talks to another." When my friend's health began

Buzz, Buzz !

to fail he bore with the long mornings and the long, long afternoons in a contemptuous silence, rousing himself at nine o'clock precisely—the hour for the taking up of the curtain in any theatre of fashion—for the long spell of talk which was his evening performance. On the last Wednesday of his life Cleever sent for me, urging that there were still some things undelivered in him, unrehearsed thoughts that I must help to cut out of the tiring brain. That evening I took for the last time my stall at his bedside.

"Grimaldi or no Grimaldi," he began, "the comedian has no right to private emotions. He takes the mask as the disappointed young women of French comedy take the veil—for good. . . . Every young actress," he went on after a pause, "should learn by heart the rehearsal scene in Goncourt's *La Faustin*. How does it go?

> Au défaut de ton bras prête-moi ton épée ;
> Donne.

Mais je ne peux pas cependant aller chercher votre épée sous votre tunique. Le geste est pour moi horriblement difficile . . . il faut que par votre position . . . vous me fournissiez un mouvement—qui ne soit ni un mouvement commun ni un mouvement canaille ! . . .[1]

---

[1] "Since your arm avails not, give me your sword."

"But surely you see that I cannot fumble for your sword in the folds of your tunic . . . the whole movement is very difficult for me . . . you must be in such a position that the gesture which is most natural to me shall be neither common nor . . . objectionable."

As the words *commun* and *canaille* are used interchangeably by many French-speaking English people, it may not be out of place to remark that to the French mind they mean quite different things. *Commun* is our English word

Epilogue

"What actresses have we nowadays who know that a gesture can be 'commun' or 'canaille'? It isn't so much that our young actresses can neither walk nor talk as that they don't know of the existence of any art of walking and talking. . . . The nice mind and the feeling heart have no more to do with the art of acting than with the turning of a barrel-organ. . . . I don't say that Phèdre must be a drab and Priola a *dépravé*, but I do say that they must have the *flair* for that sort of thing. . . ."

A few nodules of an ultimate spleen I shall tabulate :

The latest phase of the Theatre in England is adding nothing to the grace of life. But it is making *sagesse* and the writings of H. G. Wells harder to get away from.

The French are quite right to call a man who does not take life seriously a " comédien." No comedian is concerned properly with his own life at all.

No actress can play Phèdre without some inkling of the

"common," in the sense in which the commercial traveller, the insurance agent, and the photographer in Sir A. W. Pinero's *Letty* are common, the sense in which, as a class, these people *are* common, shine they never so brightly with Nature's individual polish. *Canaille* is the quality of an orange-girl promoted to the stage by virtue of beauty and low cunning. A certain amount of brains and a point of malice are essential. A fish-wife who is common may also be *canaille*—if she have the wit ; a great lady can be *canaille* if she have the malice. Mesdames Bardell, Gummidge, and Barkis were healthily common (bless 'em), Mrs. Nickleby faintly so, " Hamlet's Aunt " and Mrs. Merdle monumentally endowed, but the presiding goddess of the quality is and always will be the breathless, good-hearted, and overpowering Flora. Rosa Dartle, on the other hand, was *canaille*, but, we are given to understand, through no fault of her own. We might regard Becky Sharp as the very genius of *canaillerie* were it not for the rival claims of Valérie Marneffe (*La Cousine Bette*) and the Marquise de Merteuil (*Les Liaisons Dangereuses*).

Buzz, Buzz !

sadique en amour. But then without that neither can she play anything else.

" Why don't you pass the mustard ? " can be as terrible as " I'll chop her into messes," only it takes an actor to do it. Perhaps that is a definition of acting !

Those were the days of the real theatre when the *critique au monocle* could send his mistress to the play. Nowadays the critic makes a point of looking in himself.

" Eh, petite, veux-tu un conseil ? Trouve vite un mécreant d'amant qui te batte . . . et que tu aimes . . . ça te donnera peut-être le *la* du rôle." [1] The great book on the *la* of the theatre in England is still to be written. But the English theatre has had no *la* to write about since Ellen Terry.

What English actress knows, as every French actress knows, that the word that we wring from women in adoring them is the same the assassin chokes from them ? That's in Goncourt; but then everything the " serious " actress ought to know is in Goncourt.

Passion in the French theatre is not the respectable English thing it is in ours, a Meredithean jumble of earth and root, sap and flower, the kind of thing we forgive or make allowance for because it goes on in our back-gardens.

When your Citizen-Manager gets hold of a stick he does not try to make an actor of him. He puts the Naughty Boy into a corner with a volume of Nietzsche and a promise to let him out when he is more of a . . . Citizen.

Ask your Puritan for a list of the essential qualifications

---

[1] " My dear, let me give you a piece of advice. Look out at once for a brute of a lover who will thrash you . . . and let him be a man you are fond of . . . and then perhaps you will be able to get *inside* your rôle."

of a great actress. He will write you out a " reference " for a Nursery-Governess.

Repertory acting is not acting. It is brawling in a place of amusement.

And that is all. Now I think it will be admitted by a hater of Cleever and all his kind, even by a Lord Mayor-Elect with the fervour of office new upon him, that in dying Cleever did a citizen-like thing. He died ! There was no shilly-shallying about it. He died ! Perhaps it will not mar that achievement that the manner of his dying was quite the most artistic thing he ever did. He literally gave up his life to satisfy a fellow-artist's craving for self-expression ; and greater love of art can no man have than this. It had always been a pet grievance of Cleever's that never, never, never had he met the one other ruthless, inveterate Non-Citizen that surely the world must hold. Earnest young dramatists, decent - minded young actors courting that old beldam the Theatre from the safe shelter of their homes . . . these people he had always felt in his bones were not artists. They were Puritans, earnestly concocting and eagerly simulating in an orgy of broad-minded Citizenship. But now Cleever was to meet his match. I regret not having taken pains to elaborate round my story such an atmosphere of the sick-room as should have persuaded you, my readers, to take its tragic ending seriously. Hum to yourselves the opening bars of Strauss's " Tod und Verklärung " and you will

Buzz, Buzz !

be something in the mood. During our talks, or rather during Cleever's talking, I often found myself watching the old woman who nursed him. She took a malicious, semi-ghoulish pleasure in her ministering. "Herbalist by profession, harpy by instinct, and a great artist !" Cleever outlined her. "An unerring *flair* for the 'interesting events' of the village, a perfect nose for its deaths. The beginning and the end, she attends 'em both with equal gusto." As Cleever's illness drew to a close, I began to detect in the hag a curious impatience. "It's Martha Goodbody," Cleever explained. "She's 'expecting,' as they say, and the old girl itches to get me off her hands first. We might clash ! . . . It's a comfort to have a great artist about you," he went on; "she won't hesitate to put the pillows over one if it's her only way out." To my gesture of horror, "And why shouldn't she ? I'll chop her into messes"—this with a glint of fun—"if she isn't as 'serious' about her profession as a little bit of virtuosity like that amounts to."

As it turned out, that was Cleever's "curtain." I left him a few minutes later. Late that night I heard of his sudden passing, followed within the hour by Martha Goodbody's little affair. They told me that at the latter performance the old lady was not quite at her best. A trifle less self-possessed than usual, they thought, a shade hesitant. Whatever hand she had in Cleever's passing—which we shall never know—I am perfectly certain in

my own mind that he " offered no resistance," as
they say, and " went quietly." Her statement
was to the effect that at about one o'clock in the
morning she " noticed a change come over him,"
and that he had fallen back saying something which
sounded like " Hullo, hullo ! " This " Hullo,
hullo ! " mystified many people, but for my own
part I know it to have been a reminiscence of the
O La ! O La ! Bobby ! of Dicky Suett. Cleever
had a passion for Elia. Come to think of it, *O La !
O La !* is, if not the windiest, at least the wisest
criticism of life and death to be found in the philo-
sophies.

And the moral ? The very question would show
that I have failed. I set out to define and determine
Cleever, but from that defining and determining
to justifying or even explaining there is the whole
world, the whole of my writer's world, that is. I
set out to resolve this temperament of Cleever's
into the cosmopolitanism of his forbears—their
dignity, nonchalance even, sustained by Beethoven's
Sonatas, in the mean grip of poverty ; their pre-
occupation in circumstances of ease with those same
Sonatas. (You are to interpret the word Sonata
in its most general, unlimited, and covering sense.)
I set out to show Cleever's temperament as the
result of breeding, environment, and the inculcation
from earliest years of the doctrine of morning scales
as the first duty of man. " You needn't wash, but
don't forget to say your prayers," says an old shrew
to her grandchild in one of Sir A. W. Pinero's

Buzz, Buzz !

plays. From the age of six Cleever was left to decide for himself in the matter of devotion ; he was turned twenty before he was allowed to use his own judgment as to the running of scales.

I would not have it supposed that I am defending Cleever or that he was ever anxious to be defended. I agree that " Art for Art's sake " is a depressing, barren, and out-moded doctrine. I am not sure that a long course of the nobler and duller novels of H. G. Wells has not persuaded me that the doctrine is an entirely damnable one. In this mood I am all for a bill for the prevention of cottage pianos and the closing of art galleries and public libraries. For you cannot have art without artists ; neither can you have little artists without the disquieting big ones. " Against the blown rose will they stop their nose that kneeled unto the bud." The full-grown, a-moral artist is really a terrible nuisance.

I remember Cleever's instancing what ordinary people would call the major misfortunes of a career as examples of the " rebound " of the artistic temper. The day when Cleever lost the greater part of his fortune—a trumpery *material* happening which I have not thought worth mentioning—was also the day of his first " notice " of a great French actress ; discovery of the absence of all fineness in his relations with his mistress went hand in hand with the discovery of a fresh lilt and expressiveness in a line of *Macbeth* :

> Light *thickens,* and the crow
> Makes wing to the rooky wood.

Epilogue

" *C'est payé*," said Cleever to himself on each occasion ; " on balance I am to the good."

Against this unreason, if you like to call it so, sensible, prosaic argument is of no avail. It is Lamb's case of the rogue all over again, but with a subtle difference. That it is worth while being cheated out of a legacy to get " the idea of " the rogue who cheated you was, after all, not a very extraordinary discovery. Cleever would have preferred the more startling find that it is worth while *being* a rogue if it helps you to a fuller smack of " the taste of " roguery.

It is the case once again of the English king, " ruined, weary, with death waiting in the next room, still toiling at the attainment of a perfect, because perfectly expressed, apprehension of such flat dregs as are left him of life, still following passionately on the old quest of the ideal word, the unique image, the one perfect way of saying the one thing."

It is the case of the wretch with the rope round his neck finding interest in the tell-tale cut of his executioner's coat, in the indifferent technique of the whining priest.

Hear in yet other words and for the last time Cleever's trumpet-tongued defiance of us all. I have taken the passage from the dusty files of old journals, but the words seem to me still to possess a certain glow. " To the artist has been given the power of seeing all those things which God in His wisdom has created. The power of seeing, not of judging ; of interpreting, not mending. He is the beholder, indifferently with God, of all that there is in humanity. To him, therefore, there can only be ' the idea of ' patriotism, and not the setting of one nation above another, ' the idea of strife ' and not the espousal of particular causes."

"To the artist there can only be *patterns* in thought and action, not one virtue better than another vice."

Hear, finally, his proud rejection of our tentative apology for him and his kind. " We exist, and we claim to be immune from defence as from attack. We are, and it is mere irrelevance to argue that such existence is a bane or a blessing to ourselves or to mankind. We are, and no more to be explained away than simple-minded Cabinet Ministers or imaginative, defaulting stockbrokers. Why won't people realise—and by ' realise ' I mean feel as a revelation—that the artist is like the plain man in that he is the sole master of his destiny, that he is not to be affected other than adversely by the acceptance of any other person's code of thought or rule of conduct ? This applies from the big things like getting up in the morning to the little ones such as a belief or disbelief in the supremacy of the British Empire, from the preference for an opera down to getting married. No one can help but many are willing to hinder. All the actions and reactions which go to make up a man's entity, be he artist or simpleton, are not positive, but relative to an unknown quantity—himself, about whom the only certain thing is that he is not some one else.

234

Epilogue

Man's aim in life is to realise this lonely self of his, and in little things and in big things to try to bring it to some sort of completion.

"Men who have realised this have gone to the stake for an ideal, others have resigned themselves to pub-crawling in the evenings. I do not suppose that anybody except Ibsen has ever realised that the one is fulfilling his destiny as completely as the other. Judge not " — he would round off his little lecture with a smile — " lest ye be beside the point ! "

It is significant that in the admirable collection of books left by Cleever and which afterwards came to me, there is to be found one pencilled passage, and one only. The marked lines are in Masefield's *The Everlasting Mercy* :

> Perhaps when man has entered in
> His perfect city free from sin,
> The campers will come past the walls
> With old lame horses full of galls,
> And waggons hung about with withies,
> And burning coke in tinker's stithies,
> And see tne golden town and choose,
> And think the wild too good to lose,
> And camp outside as these camped then
> With wonder at the entering men.

In the margin, in fine handwriting, are the words *Très bien !*

It is characteristic of Cleever that he should have preferred the French.